Dinner's Ready!

Recipes for Working Moms

Dinner's Ready!

Recipes for Working Moms

Rebecca Cailor

atmosphere press

This book is dedicated to Mike, my husband, and Mike and Yadira Eberhardt for their support in this endeavor.

Table of Contents

International Favorites

Secret Sauces

Introduction

I started writing this book because a working mother has less time to care for her children than a stay-at-home parent. The working mother does laundry, helps with homework, and cooks and packs meals and lunches, and on the rare day off, she has to entertain her children and help with school projects. The statistics show that over 50% of the United States workforce is working females who have children. In America, 80% of women are working, whether married or not. As a single parent, I realized how hard it was to make nutritious meals quickly after work and make something my kids could use for healthy and tasty lunches. With the fast pace of working and raising children, time is of the essence.

I started cooking when I was going through nursing school, working as a certified nursing assistant on weekends, and raising a one- and three-year-old by myself. Recently divorced, raising children by yourself, and going to school is really two or three jobs. I also had a house that had to be remodeled to make it livable. While I was working two jobs and raising children, I finally came up with the three rules of motherhood: "I don't do guilt; Life is not always fair; and I am not here to just entertain you. I am here to provide you with healthy home-cooked meals with an abundance of love." My oldest son repeated this to his friend when he was trying to guilt me into taking them somewhere. He looked right at him and said the rules.

Cooking different cultural dishes became a necessity due to a very limited budget. There are international recipes which are in a separate chapter. Some of these take longer than 30 minutes, so they could not be included, but some are staples that can be frozen and used quickly when needed, e.g., Real Italian Meatballs. I have collected 30-minute recipes from many people and many countries in the last 40 years. So, this recipe book has an international and personal twist to it. I have been remarried for the last 28 years, and we jokingly state that my cooking experiments might have killed my first husband. However, my present husband is a foodie with corporate experience in the food arena, and my best critic.

The first international cuisine that I made for some of my nurse buddies was from a Chinese cookbook. Since then, I have added Thai, Italian, Malaysian, German, North American, and Caribbean cuisines. There are many frozen meals available now that did not exist 50 years ago, but they still come in smaller portions, with too much salt and lots of preservatives. My recipes only use natural ingredients and taste better than most store-bought brands. My oldest son was allergic to butter, so I had to be creative. These recipes are amazing and created to give your children a variety of tastes and flavors so they can adapt easily to other cultures, and these foods are very nutritious. The fish and seafood recipes are what I call "brain food," especially healthy for teenagers who are developing their brains. Some of my recipes are handed down, and some I learned overseas. For those who have allergies or do not eat meat, a few of my recipes are totally vegan and gluten free. I hope you and your family enjoy these recipes.

30-Minute Recipes

I have collected these recipes during my lifetime to save you time. Working moms do not have a lot of time when they get home and there are tips and tricks in these recipes that will help. Some are Italian, a few are my sons' favorites, and others are from different parts of the world. The spices in these dishes are very basic and you can find them in the grocery stores. The Chicken Fricassee with Biscuits is a North American classic and very tasty. The prep and cooking time should be no more than 30 minutes which makes it easier to cook and more time to spend with your family.

5-Minute Garlic Bread

This is the quickest way to broil the perfect garlic bread, unless you buy it already prepared. I have tried some of the prepared garlic breads, but sometimes they use oleo and other buttery flavored fats. The bread can be soggy if they use different fats. By making garlic bread at home, you'll always know what ingredients are in your bread.

Ingredients:
1-2 loaves French bread or 12 bread rolls
1 stick butter, at room temperature
½ tsp garlic salt, sprinkled lightly

Directions: Preheat oven on broil and put oven rack on second level from the top, about 4-6 inches from the broiler flame. Cut bread longwise in half using a bread knife. Spread butter in a light layer on both open halves of bread and lay buttered side up on a large cookie sheet. Sprinkle bread with a little garlic salt. If you want Parmesan garlic bread, sprinkle dried Parmesan cheese on the top of the bread last. Put under broiler for 4-5 minutes. Toast should be brown on the edges and perfectly warm. If it burns, it is too close to the broiler flame. Serves 6-8 people.

Broiled Butterfly Shrimp

This is one of my sons' favorites. If you want to make it low fat, you can use margarine or olive oil instead of butter. This recipe is super simple and packed with protein for your kids. It is easy and takes five minutes in the broiler. The recipe for shrimp cocktail is in the chapter for secret sauces. The taste of this dish depends on the type of shrimp you buy. If it is fresh and not frozen, you are blessed. In the high desert we only have frozen shrimp, and I prefer Argentinian shrimp if I buy it frozen. The colder water makes it taste less fishy.

Ingredients:
2 lbs fresh or frozen large or jumbo shrimp, deveined, uncooked
1 stick butter or margarine
2 tsps. Old Bay seasoning

Directions: If the shrimp is frozen with or without tails, you can thaw it quickly by opening the bag and pouring hot water directly into the bag to thaw and wash it at the same time. You can leave the tails on or pull them off when they are thawed. Run a small sharp knife down the back of each shrimp, on the outside of the curve.

This will make them open fillets.Put a sheet of foil on a cookie sheet to catch the butter. This helps in cleanup. Lay the open fillets of shrimp flat on the foil, in two or three rows, opening the shrimp to expose more surface area. Melt the stick of butter or margarine in a microwaveable small bowl (usually just 20-30 seconds—if you leave butter in the microwave for too long, like a minute, the butter will explode.) Pour the melted butter in a line over the shrimp rows. Sprinkle Old Bay seasoning on top. Turn oven broiler on. Put the cookie sheet with shrimp on the lowest rack so it does not flame. Leave in broiler for 5 minutes. Shrimp is done when the flesh has turned white. This is ready to eat after 5 minutes of broiling. You can put them on skewers with pineapple or eat them with a fork as they are. Serves 4 people.

Broiled Salmon (or fresh fish of your choice)

This is a quick meal that is very nutritious with lots of omega-3 fatty acids in it. It's good for your heart and good for your brain. All of us know that teenagers need omega-3 fatty acids and protein for their heart and brain development. If you have leftovers, there is another quick recipe in this chapter for Salmon Salad that works well for another meal.

Ingredients:
1 ½ - 2 lb salmon fillet, thawed
1 tsp fresh ground or cracked pepper
½ tsp Old Bay seasoning
½ tsp garlic salt

Directions: Set oven on broil. Nobody likes to clean broiler pans, so put foil on top of a regular sized cookie sheet to make cleanup easier. Put the salmon fillet skin side down on the foil-covered cookie sheet. Mix seasonings and sprinkle on top of the fillet. Cook on broil for 15-25 minutes. Salmon is done when the white fat has drained out and the center is no longer dark pink. Overcooking it will make it too dry. Peel salmon off of the foil with a spatula for serving. The skin will stick to the foil, and you can throw it away (unless you have cats). Serves 4 people.

Cajun Jambalaya

This is a traditional Caribbean dish and great for leftovers. The longest part of the preparation is just waiting for the rice to cook. It is a great dish for leftover grilled chicken or sausages. I use shrimp, but you can use just about any meat. In fact, in Louisiana, they commonly use crawfish and crab, as well as Andouille sausage for the spice. You can add more Cajun spice and/or hot peppers if you like it spicier. I have one son who likes super spicy and one who doesn't—that's the way children are. This seems to satisfy them both. One large frying pan makes a large batch and can serve 5-6 people easily.

Ingredients:
1 lb shrimp without the tails, cleaned
1 lb chicken, already cooked and cubed
1 lb smoked sausage or cut up links
1 cup rice
1 cup tomato sauce
1/4 tsp Cajun spice
1 tbsp garlic salt
1 tbsp chili powder
1 red pepper, diced
3 tbsp olive oil
2 cups hot water

Directions: In your largest frying pan, add all ingredients above with oil, except for the rice and water. If you do not have a large frying pan, you can use a 4-quart kettle. Cook until shrimp is done and pepper is soft, about 5-10 minutes, over medium heat. Add 1 cup of rice and 2 cups of hot water and stir into mixture of meats and spices. Cover and cook for 20 minutes or until rice is done. Stir well. Serves 6 people.

Caribbean Coconut Curried Chicken

This is an easy dish and quick to make. If you have a child with a sweet tooth, it is perfect. My youngest son is a seafood monster and would eat this by the ton. You can add more curry if you like it spicier, or leave it as is if you like it sweeter.

Ingredients:
4 tbsp olive oil
2 [8 oz] cans coconut cream (not coconut milk)
2 tbsp corn starch (for thickener)
2 lbs chicken breasts
1 tsp yellow curry
1 tsp salt
½ tsp pepper
Fresh coconut, out of the shell, cut up into small chunks
1 cup rice
2 cups boiling water

Directions: Start boiling water and add rice, reducing heat to simmer and cover for twenty minutes. While rice is cooking, add oil in large frying pan with a lid. Cut chicken breasts up in 2- to 3-inch slices, then cook in oil on medium heat until chicken is done. Add seasonings and curry and stir in coconut cream and corn starch for thickening. Add coconut chunks. Cook 15-20 minutes, until mixture is the thickness of gravy and well heated. Serve over rice, which should be done at the same time as the sauce is thickening. Serves 4-6 people.

Caribbean Fried Bananas

You can use plantains or bananas for this dish. This is a yummy dish that you can serve for dessert with caramel sauce or just eat plain. This is used a lot in the Caribbean for breakfast. It is full of potassium. It is also full of tryptophan, guaranteed to put everyone to sleep. Sometimes that is a nice break for a working mom or dad. If the bananas are *almost* ripe, it is easier to cut them in slices. If using plantains, they should be completely yellow and turning black to be sweeter—when green, they can be bitter and tough.

Ingredients:
3 lbs bananas, about 4-5 large ones
2 tbsp cane sugar
1 tbsp ground cinnamon
¼ cup olive oil

Directions: Heat olive oil in a nonstick large skillet over medium high heat. Cut bananas lengthwise in two or three long slices each. Lay flat in the preheated skillet, and sprinkle with one half of the cane sugar and cinnamon. When dark brown on one side, turn the slices over and fry the other side. Sprinkle the rest of the cane sugar and cinnamon on the side that was down in the pan first. When both sides are dark brown, they are ready to serve. A little caramel sauce and whipped cream garnish makes a tasty, elegant dessert. Serves 4-6 people.

Chicken Fricassee with Biscuits

I serve this over biscuits—Southern style. It is a great recipe for leftover chicken. When I make a whole fried or baked chicken there are always leftover wings or other parts that people don't or won't eat. There won't be any leftovers with this meal, even with finnicky eaters. I use any brand of layered or flaky buttermilk biscuits that are in the grocery refrigerator section. They rise better than my made-from-scratch biscuits and are quicker.

> Ingredients:
> 2 lbs organic chicken meat, cut in ½ inch pieces
> 1 tbsp olive oil
> ½ tsp thyme
> ½ tsp garlic salt
> 1 tsp dried sage
> Pepper to taste
> 1 cup diced onions
> 1 cup diced celery
> ½ cup flour
> 3 cups water

Directions: Put refrigerator biscuits on a cookie sheet and pop in the oven at 350 degrees Fahrenheit for 20 minutes, until golden brown. While these are cooking, get a Dutch oven or 4-quart saucepan and add olive oil, seasonings, chicken, celery, and onions. Let simmer on medium heat until the onion is blanched, about 15 minutes. Stir well while heating. Then add ½ cup of flour to make the roux, stirring it into the chicken, celery, and onion until there are no white lumps left of the flour. Add 3 cups of water, stir in well, let cook on medium to low heat for 15 minutes or until the sauce is a thick gravy. Biscuits should be ready by the time the sauce is done. Ladle the chicken fricassee over a biscuit or two and serve hot. Serves 4-6.

Chili Con Carne

This is a traditional Mexican and American favorite. Unlike the Texas style chili, I like to add pinto or black beans to it. It is quick and nutritious. One thing my boys were really proud of was their gastric noise after eating chili. I like to use leftover grilled meat, which gives it a little smokey flavor, or you can use a chipotle smoked chili or a green chili for the base pepper. You can brown hamburger if you are short on time. It takes 5-10 minutes to defrost hamburger in a microwave.

Ingredients:
1 medium onion, diced
1 raw green chili pepper, diced
1 [16 oz] can stewed tomatoes
2 lbs meat, diced and cooked
3 tbsp olive oil
1 [8 oz] can black or pinto beans, drained
1/2 tsp garlic salt
2 tbsp chili powder
1 [8 oz] bag shredded cheddar

Directions: Put the diced onion and green pepper in a 2-quart saucepan with the olive oil and cook on medium low heat until the vegetables are sautéed, about 5 minutes. Add spices and remaining ingredients, and simmer on a low boil for 25 minutes. The smaller the meat is diced, the more tender it will become. Serve topped with shredded cheese, and crackers on the side. Serves 4 people.

Chinese Sweet and Sour Stir-Fry

This dish is easy and nutritious. This is one of the first cultural dishes that I introduced my kids to, because I don't know any children who don't like something a little sweet. If your meat is not defrosted first, you can defrost one or two chicken breasts in about 6 minutes on the defrost setting on a microwave. This will not cook it completely but will make it tender enough to cut up. It takes about 20 minutes for the meat to brown and the vegetables to get tender. Once in a while, I add fresh pineapple cut up in chunks, which is the Chinese Cantonese style.

Ingredients:
1 lb meat of choice, sliced (Chicken is easiest and fastest to cook. The thinner the meat is sliced, the more tender it will cook.)
1 tsp pepper
1 onion, sliced or quartered
4 tbsp olive oil
1 whole green or red pepper, chopped up in chunks
1 whole carrot, chopped up in small chunks
Recipe for sauce is under Secret Sauces Section, but I will add it here too:
½ cup honey
¼ cup soy sauce
Juice of one lemon or orange
1 pinch dried ginger

Directions: Using a large frying pan, add the chicken, pepper, and vegetables to 4 tbsp of olive oil and cover, cooking over medium-low heat until meat is brown and well cooked. Stir occasionally to prevent burning. Add the sauce ingredients once the meat and vegetables are tender but not mushy. Stir in well for flavor and serve over rice or chow mein noodles. Serves 4 people.

Coriander and Raisin Cake

This is a twist on the old chocolate cake mix. Coriander is a sweet and pungent spice, used a lot in Persian food and Indian recipes. This is another good thing to pack in lunches.

Ingredients:
1 tsp ground coriander
1 tsp cinnamon
1 chocolate cake mix
1 cup raisins

Directions: Follow the directions on the chocolate cake mix package, and once mixed, add remaining ingredients listed above. Cook according to the directions on box. Add brown sugar frosting (see chapter on Quick Desserts for recipe). Serves 8-12 people.

Crepes Suzette

This is one of my family's favorites for breakfast. It is a sweet but healthier version of pancakes. Crepes are thinner, and the fruit is fresh, making it tasty but with less sugar. If you have a child with ADHD, which I did, you already know that processed sugar will make them bounce off the walls. I prefer making my own sauce from fresh fruit, but you can use unsweetened canned cherries or canned peaches as well. The main problem people have with crepe dishes is that the crepes often stick. I have one nonstick crepe pan that my husband bought just for his favorite crepes. It keeps them from folding down or sticking. If you don't have a nonstick pan, you can use nonstick cooking spray. If you have a regular skillet, you must prepare the pan with hot oil before each crepe, and it takes longer. The nonstick olive oil cooking spray is easier and quicker to apply between crepes. I have used pancake batter, but the Belgian waffle mix has a different mixture of yeast, and if you pour the crepe thin, it does not taste like a pancake.

Ingredients:
1 cup Belgian waffle mix (or complete pancake mix)
3 raw eggs
1 ½ - 2 cups water (add until batter is thin)
1 can sweet cherry filling or 2 cups frozen fruit
1 can whipped cream

Directions: Using a nonstick medium-sized or 10-inch crepe pan, spray with nonstick cooking spray. Heat over medium flame to get the pan hot. Mix the waffle mix, 3 raw eggs, and water with a whisk or blender until smooth. Pour ¼ cup of batter into the skillet, making sure it is thin, and spread it to the edges. Flip after crepe is getting brown around the edges. Heat up canned cherry filling for one minute in the microwave. If you are using fresh frozen fruit, you can put it on a burner on medium heat and it will be hot and stewed when you are done flipping crepes. Most people can eat 3 regular crepes, so put 2 or 3 crepes in a stack on a plate. Add 3 large tablespoons of cherry filling or hot fruit medley on top. Top off with whipped cream and enjoy a French breakfast. Serves 4-5 people.

Garlic and Basil Meatloaf

Meatloaf was one of those recipes that appeared after World War II when large families finally had access to beef without limitations. It is still popular, but sometimes flavorless. I often add garlic, basil, and black olives to this recipe. If you are on a low-fat diet, you can substitute ground chicken or turkey breast for the meat. In a hurry? Use Italian breadcrumbs, which have the seasonings in them. The eggs hold it together, so there is no need for oil or extra fat.

Ingredients:
2 lbs ground hamburger, thawed
1 tsp garlic salt
2 tbsp garlic, crushed or minced
1 cup fresh basil, chopped
3 eggs
1 can sliced black olives, drained
1 cup breadcrumbs or ground up cracker crumbs

Directions: Chop up the basil first and preheat your oven to 400 degrees Fahrenheit. Add all ingredients in a large mixing bowl and mix until well blended. I use my hands to mix, after washing them. It is much easier than using a spoon or large fork. Put into a regular-sized loaf pan after spraying with nonstick cooking spray. Put in the oven on 400 degrees Fahrenheit for 25 minutes. Serves 6 people.

Gluten-Free Vegetarian Tacos

Gluten-Free Vegetarian Tacos require 15 minutes to season and heat. They are yummy and you can choose the salsa of your choice to flavor the meat. My sons would not eat vegetarian food if they knew it was vegan. This is disguised with good flavor and it's better for them. I use a certain brand of vegetarian burgers that taste the best to me. Chicken-flavored do not seem to work as well. Most vegetarian burgers are bean or rice based, and instead of lettuce, I use alfalfa sprouts, which are just as crunchy and more nutritious. My husband is a food snob and thought these were better than real hamburger tacos.

Ingredients:
4 frozen vegetable burgers (not necessary to thaw them first)
1 package alfalfa or fresh bean sprouts
3 tbsp salsa of choice (for spice and flavor)
2 tbsp olive oil
½ cup fresh cilantro
1 box [8-10] hard taco shells

Directions: Put olive oil in large frying pan, then add four vegetarian burgers in a single layer. Add all remaining ingredients, except the bean sprouts. Cook on medium-low heat, and cover for 5 minutes. Now the burgers can be chopped up into smaller pieces for tacos, stirred, covered, and heated for 15 minutes. While taco mix is heating, put 2 tablespoons of alfalfa or bean sprouts into each taco shell. Cover with the cooked mixture of vegetable burger, cilantro, and salsa. Serve while hot. Each vegetarian burger makes 2-3 tacos, depending on the size of the shells. Serves 4-5 people.

Homemade Tomato Vegetable Juice

This is similar in taste to the more expensive types of vegetable juice. The difference is that store-bought juices are loaded with salt, while you can adjust the sodium in this recipe for a low-sodium diet. It is still packed with lots of potassium and vitamins. This is a perfect blender breakfast for the "juicers" who do not have time to eat before dropping off the kids, going to work, etc., and it also makes a perfect Bloody Mary mix.

Ingredients:
1 large cucumber, diced and peeled
¼ tsp garlic salt
2 fresh large tomatoes, diced
1 green pepper, diced
Fresh ground pepper to taste
½ cup fresh cilantro, finely chopped
3 medium green onions, diced
2 cups water (use more if still too thick to pour)

Directions: Mix all ingredients in a large blender and blend on high until smooth and pureed without lumps. Saves well for 3 days if refrigerated. Makes 4 x 8 oz servings.

Homemade Granola

I get tired of the high prices on granola, which is one of my favorite hiking foods. I found out as a single parent that hiking and camping was a great way to get the kids to burn off some of their energy, and it was cheaper than the movies. They also learn something and get stronger. If you are a hiker, this is a perfectly healthy snack for your children. Up in the Sierras, when one of my children's blood sugar dropped out of sight, this snack was the perfect cure.

I learned how to make my own granola as a matter of necessity. Buying it premade is very pricey. Granola bars have as much sugar as a regular candy bar. I do not like chocolate chips in my granola, but you may add them if you like. This recipe makes a one-gallon bag, and it is healthy, lowers your cholesterol, and is packed full of fiber. Instead of raisins and cranberries, you can substitute banana chips, chopped apricots, and pineapple for the tropical version.

Ingredients:
3 cups muesli or rolled oats
½ cup sugar or sugar substitute
1 tsp ground cinnamon
1 cup raisins
1 cup dried cranberries
1 cup unsalted almonds
1 cup peanuts (if you have no allergies)

Directions: Mix all dry ingredients in a bowl, package in plastic gallon bag(s) and you are set. For a healthy dessert, this is also a yummy topping for frozen yogurt. Poor milk on it or top with yogurt, and you have a heart-happy breakfast. Fills a one-gallon storage bag.

Kosher Tabouli

This recipe was given to me by one of my close friends. You can make it spicier by substituting fresh spearmint instead of cilantro. Some kids prefer the spearmint over the cilantro. It is quick, very healthy, and easy. Bulgur wheat bulgur comes in two forms, couscous or risotto, usually found in the pasta and rice aisle.

Ingredients:
1 cup couscous
2 cups boiling water
1 tsp garlic salt
1 whole tomato, diced
1 bunch cilantro or 1 cup mint leaves, chopped fine
1 cup green onions, diced
¼ cup vinegar
3 tbsp olive oil

Directions: Boil 2 cups of water. While waiting for water to boil, start chopping up the tomato, cilantro, and green onions. Add couscous or bulgur wheat to boiling water. Add one tablespoon of olive oil to this now, so it does not stick and get lumpy. Cover and remove from heat.

Once bulgur has cooked (about 5 minutes), add remaining olive oil, salt, diced green onions, cilantro or mint, vinegar, and chopped tomato. Stir until well mixed. You can leave this in the refrigerator to chill. It makes a nice side salad, or you can serve it with pita bread. Serves 4-6 people.

Mexican Tostadas

These are easy to make and nutritious. I learned to make these in Texas in the '70s, when I was in the military, from a chef at Night in Old San Antonio (NISOA). You can buy tostada shells, but they are much fresher and crisper if you use old corn tortillas. I use this recipe for leftover beef (carne asada) or leftover pork (carnitas).

Ingredients:
For tostadas:
2 cups oil in a large frying pan
12 corn tortillas
For carne asada or carnitas filling:
2 cups leftover beef or pork
1 can refried beans (black or pintos)
2 tbsp salsa flavor of choice
1 tomato, diced
½ tsp salt
1 cup lettuce, shredded
1 cup low-fat cheese, shredded

Directions: To prepare your meat filling, you must cut the meat really thin so it is more tender, in ½ inch pieces. Put the diced meat, diced tomato, salsa, and salt in a 1-quart saucepan and simmer on low heat until the meat falls apart with a fork. While the meat is cooking, open the can of refried beans and put in a glass bowl in the microwave for 2 minutes. Stir well and add salt and salsa to flavor if you prefer. Some canned refried beans have spices already in them.

For fresh tostada shells, cook the oil on medium high in a large skillet. Depending on the size of your frying pan, lay 2 to 4 tortillas flat and turn them over when they are golden brown. This takes 1-2 minutes. If your oil is too hot, it will smoke. If it is too cold, it will take longer. When they are golden brown, remove from heat with tongs (I use my steel tongs) and put the tostadas on paper towels to absorb any excess oil.

Add a thin layer of refried beans to the surface of the tostada shells, and top with 2 or 3 tablespoons of the meat mixture that should be done by now. Top with shredded cheese, shredded lettuce, and extra fresh cilantro if you like. This makes 2-3 tostadas per person, so 12 tostadas will serve 4-6 people.

Poached Cod

This is an easy, healthy dish that I especially like with cod. You could use tilapia or other fish, but cod is quick and tastes less "fishy." Do not use lemon juice substitute—it does not taste the same due to the preservative potassium sorbate.

Ingredients:
2 lbs fresh or frozen cod fillets
3 tbsp olive oil
1 whole fresh lemon
1 cup white wine
Salt and pepper to taste
1 tsp dried dill

Directions: Slice lemon up into ¼ inch slices with a sharp knife. Put lemon slices flat on the bottom of a large skillet. Add olive oil to prevent sticking. Put fresh or frozen fish fillets on top of the lemon slices. Sprinkle with salt, pepper, and dried dill. Cover and cook on medium-low heat for 20-30 minutes. Cod is done when the fish flakes easily with a fork and is opaque white in color. Lift out with a spatula and serve while hot. Serves 4 people at ½ fillet or ½ pound per person.

Italian Marsala Spaghetti Sauce

This is a makeshift dish, and you can use prepared spaghetti sauce as your base or use a 16 ounce can of stewed tomatoes. My youngest son likes my spaghetti and meatballs so much that he makes yum yum noises when he eats them and his head rocks sideways. If you are on a salt restricted diet, you do not want to use spaghetti sauce from a jar, as it has lots of salt. I keep fresh basil and diced green peppers in the freezer. If you freeze your fresh herbs, the leaves come off in the freezer, and the stems are all left in the freezer bag. They still taste fresher than dried herbs.

Ingredients:
1 jar or can spaghetti
sauce or stewed
tomatoes
1 tbsp crushed garlic
(available in the
produce section of most grocery stores)
1 green pepper, diced
(see Glossary section for pre-freezing)
1 can diced black olives (if you prefer olives with your sauce)
2 tbsp olive oil

½ cup fresh basil leaves, chopped
¼ tsp black ground pepper
Grated Parmesan for garnish

Directions: Put the olive oil, garlic, chopped basil, and diced green peppers in a 2-quart pan, and heat on medium until the green peppers are soft. Add the can or jar of prepared spaghetti sauce as the base and cook on low until well mixed and heated. You can add dried red-hot peppers if you like it Sicilian style and spicy. Add chopped black olives if you prefer them. Serve over pasta and/or meatballs. I like to serve it with 5-minute garlic bread, with or without Parmesan cheese. Serves 4-6 people.

Real Italian Meatball Sandwiches

These have less preservatives than some of the fast-food varieties, so they are better for you. This recipe is one of my husband's favorites—he especially likes them packed for lunch. These can be served warmed or cold (see Real Italian Meatballs in International Recipes Section). I usually make a dozen meatballs beforehand, which can be refrigerated for up to 10 days, and frozen if needed. One dozen will not last a whole week in my house, as there seems to be a meatball troll who eats them in the middle of the night. You can serve the sandwiches with pasta sauce or plain, if you are packing them, so they do not get soggy.

Ingredients:
4 hamburger buns or toasted hoagie buns
4 Italian 3" meatballs
1 large tomato
Catsup and mayonnaise or pasta sauce

Directions: Toast buns in toaster oven on one side. Apply one tsp of catsup on 4 tops, and one tsp of mayonnaise on 4 bun bottoms. Slice tomato in thin slices and put one slice on the mayonnaise side. Cut meatballs in half, layer on buns, and close. You can add lettuce and avocado or marsala sauce if you like, but I am giving you just the basics. Serves 4 meatball sandwiches.

Shrimp Alfredo

This is a classic Italian dish and so easy to make if you are short on time. If you have shellfish allergies, you can used cubed chicken breasts as an alternate meat. If you have finnicky eaters, they might like anything with cheese sauce on it—that is how I disguised vegetables like broccoli. Apparently, children like the cheese more than the food it is on. I like this recipe because you can add frozen meats once you make the sauce. There is no need to add salt if you use shrimp and Parmesan cheese. If you use chicken, add ½ tsp of garlic salt.

Ingredients:
½ cup powdered Parmesan cheese
2 tbsp garlic, crushed
½ tsp ground black pepper
2 tbsp olive oil
1 lb pasta noodles (angel hair or spaghetti are preferable)
1-1/2 lb shrimp, clean, frozen, and de-tailed
1 cup milk

Directions: Before you cook the sauce, heat a large pan of water for the pasta, and add the pasta when it is boiling. Turn down on low for 10 minutes. Rinse shrimp off with warm water. Heat olive oil and garlic in a skillet on medium heat to give more flavor to the garlic. Add powdered Parmesan, black pepper, and milk while stirring constantly. Once sauce has no lumps, add shrimp and let cook until it is boiling. Drain the noodles and put in a bowl. Pour alfredo sauce over the whole bowl or divide the noodles into individual portions and pour the sauce on each portion. Serves 6.

Smoked Salmon Wrap

This is a slight twist on bagels and lox, and a whole lot easier to make. You can use light sour cream or cream cheese for the inside of the wrap. I prefer sour cream because it is easier to apply to a tortilla. These take about 15 minutes to prepare. The hardest part is slicing the tomato and onion. They pack well for lunches. Smoked salmon, like any fish, provides teenagers omega-3 oils for their heart and brain function. Teenagers need more "brain food"—I just wish it could counteract their raging hormones.

Ingredients:
1 package of flour tortillas
1 [8 oz] package of smoked salmon lox (slices)
1 head lettuce
1 tomato, sliced
½ medium onion, sliced
1 cup sour cream

Directions: Lay fresh flour tortillas on a counter or preparation area that has been cleaned. Apply two tablespoons of sour cream in the center of the tortillas in a long line, using a table knife. Lay two small slices of salmon longways on the center of the tortilla. Add two or three long shreds of lettuce on top, one slice of onion, and one slice of tomato. Roll up like a burrito with the ends tucked in. Makes 8 rolls. Serves 4-6 people, depending on their appetite.

Southern Ham and Cheese Corn Pone

This is a post-Revolutionary War dish from American history. It is still made in the South and originated from pure need. After the Revolutionary War, the fields were burned, and the cattle and pigs were stolen. After the Civil War, the dried corn and smoked meat was the main meal because it had been kept hidden in the barn or in the cellar. Dried corn soaked in water over low heat was turned into hominy or ground up. This dish was also made from pure need in my home. My children probably never knew they ate this and brown beans for three days one time because my paycheck was late. That is when I learned to buy a little more than I needed with my paycheck and to stock a larder. Grits and cornbread are made from corn. The cheese is added to give it a more scrumptious flavor, and this recipe works well with leftovers of a holiday ham.

Ingredients:
4 cups or two large [16 oz] cans hominy
2 cups water
1 ½ cups whipped vegetable shortening
3 cups smoked cooked ham, diced
2 cups shredded cheddar or American cheese
1 tsp black pepper
1 tsp salt

Directions: Preheat the oven to 350 degrees Fahrenheit. Heat the hominy, water, and shortening on medium until the shortening is melted. While the mixture is warm, put in a blender and puree. (This beats the heck out of using a mixer.) Add remaining ingredients and pour into casserole dish. Let cook for 35 minutes, or until the top is golden brown. Feeds 6-8 people.

Spanish Refried Beans

Beans are a staple in almost every country around the equator. Refried beans are simple to cook, and with the grocery beans that are already cooked in a can, it does not take all day. These can be made as spicy as you want them, or mild, but the pepper, onion, and tomato give the frijoles a little more flavor. You can serve them alone, as a side, or with tortilla chips. As a bean dip, they are much healthier than the store-bought dip with preservatives—a perfect football or party favorite.

Ingredients:
2 cans cooked black or pinto beans
1 medium tomato, diced
1 small onion, diced
1 green pepper, diced (you can use a chili or sweet pepper depending on your taste buds)
1 tsp chili powder
½ tsp garlic salt
2 tbsp olive oil

Directions: Put all ingredients except beans in a 2-quart saucepan and cook on medium heat for 15 minutes to sauté vegetables in olive oil. Drain the juice out of canned beans while waiting for the vegetables to cook. Add drained beans, cover, and simmer for 15 minutes until boiling. Using a potato masher or hand mixer, blend or squash all ingredients until smooth. Serve with tortilla chips. Serves 4-6 people.

Steamers in Clam Broth

This is a New England favorite and a super easy dish to make if you have access to fresh clams. I have one son who is a real seafood hound. He could eat 2 pounds of steamers by himself. The French bread is for dipping into the broth, which is full of Italian spices and garlic. It is a quick meal for a cool winter night. Some larger food chains also sell clams already shucked or shelled in 2-quart cans. Those are ideal and just need to be rinsed, reserving the juice for the broth.

Ingredients:
2 loaves French bread
3 lbs clams, washed and shucked
4 cups water
3 tbsp garlic, minced
2 tsp garlic salt
1 whole onion, diced
1 stick butter (1/2 cup)
2 tsp oregano
2 tsp dried basil
1 cup white wine

Directions: Put the clams (without the water) together with the salt, butter, diced onion, garlic, wine, and spices in a 4-quart kettle. Cook on medium heat for 5-10 minutes, until butter is well melted and onion is soft. This makes the roux for the clam broth base. If the clams are canned, you can add the broth or clam juice from the can once the roux is made. If the clams are fresh, add 4 cups of water and cook on medium-high heat for 20 minutes, stirring occasionally. Serve hot in large bowls, with a slice or two of French bread on the side. Bon appetit! Serves 4 people.

Strike-Stew Casserole

This casserole comes with a variety of names. On the East Coast of North America, it was called strike stew in the '40s because it would serve a whole family and was cheap to make when unions were fighting for workers' rights. Union pay was less than $20 a week when the workers were on strike, and many union members had large families to feed. Therefore, this is a great recipe to help stretch the family budget when you have a pound of hamburger left.

Ingredients:
½ lb elbow macaroni
1 lb hamburger or ground meat
1 [8 oz] can tomato sauce
1 medium onion, diced
1 tsp black pepper
1 tsp salt
1 tsp basil
½ tsp oregano
1 cup Parmesan or cheddar cheese, shredded (optional)

Directions: Preheat oven to 400 degrees Fahrenheit. Brown and chop up the hamburger in a large frying pan while the macaroni is boiling in a 2-quart pot. Add spices while the hamburger is cooking on medium heat in the frying pan. Once hamburger is cooked, add onion, tomato sauce, and macaroni. Macaroni does not have to be totally done—it is fine if it is partially cooked. Pour into a large casserole dish sprayed with nonstick cooking spray. I use an oblong 6"x12" casserole dish, but it will fill a large bowl as well. Bake until the top is brown and starting to crisp on the edges. Add cheese to the top if you like. Bake at 400 degrees Fahrenheit about 30 minutes. Serves 6-8 people.

Vegan Parmesan Portobellos

This is an easy and nutritious Italian dish, perfect for those who love Parmesan cheese and like mushrooms.

Ingredients:
6 average fresh portobello mushrooms
½ cup garlic mixed with softened butter
½ cup Parmesan cheese, powdered or fresh grated

Directions: Wash portobello mushrooms and take the stems out, leaving the bottoms or caps whole. Put portobellos on a cookie sheet, bottoms up. Put one teaspoon of garlic butter in the center of each portobello cap. Spoon grated or powdered cheese into the center of each cap. Sprinkle with a little pepper on top. Put the tray on the middle rack in the oven and broil the tops for about 10 minutes or until the cheese is golden brown. Serves 4-6, depending on the size of the mushrooms.

Vietnamese Spring Rolls

These are one of my favorites for summertime, as they are light and nutritious. The peanut sauce used for dipping gives the rolls a little spicy kick when used with fresh lettuce and mint leaves. If you have peanut allergies, you can use Mae Ploy or Asian sweet dipping sauce. For my son that likes spicy, I would use peanut sauce. For the other son, Mae Ploy for the sweet tooth (see Secret Sauces chapter to create your own). You can use shrimp or chicken slices that are cooked, depending on your preference and if your kids have shellfish allergies. If you grow your own mint, it is even better for you. The peanut sauce and round rice paper wraps are usually found in the Asian food section of a grocery store. It may take a little practice to make the spring rolls look nice without tears or defects. My first attempt at rolling these resembled something like rolls; tasty, but not exactly oblong and smooth.

Ingredients:
1 lb cooked and cleaned jumbo shrimp without tails, or 1
    lb thinly sliced, cooked chicken (great use for leftover
    chicken breasts)
1 package thin rice paper round sheets
1 small head fresh lettuce (the crunchier the better)
1 bunch fresh spearmint leaves
1 cup peanut sauce or sweet sauce (if allergic to peanuts)

Directions: If you are using cooked shrimp, you will have to butterfly fillet them in half to fit in the rolls. Just cut the shrimp longways down the middle, without the tails. If you use chicken, cut it in long, thin strips. First, gently moisten three individual rice paper circles on both sides and lay each one flat and separately on a clean counter or preparation area.

I usually make two or three at a time. If you wet them all and they sit for too long, they get sticky and will not peel off of the counter. Place two or three long strips of lettuce in the center of each wrap. Add one or two mint leaves on top, and then two flat pieces of the shrimp or chicken. Roll up into a closed-end roll like a burrito. Serve on a cold plate. Serves 8 people.

International Favorites

These are recipes that are served in restaurants, and some of these I learned from restaurant owners, their sons, and family members. Traveling opens new horizons in cuisine. If you approach most chefs with curiosity and the openness of a little child, they are glad to share their secrets with somebody who appreciates their food. I try to learn the basics of a language of a country about 3 months prior to traveling, which gives me enough time to ask some of my multicultural friends how to say certain things and helps when shopping. Numbers and foods are a must for traveling. Some of the chefs would make me promise to send them some American spices that they could not get in their own country. Some would barter for chocolate. One lady who made my husband and me a beautiful stew-fish with homemade bread in the Caribbean asked for a specific kind of chocolate in return. I sent her two pounds.

(Low-fat) Bom-Bom Wontons

This is a recipe that I have used for many years after being taught how to wrap them correctly by my ex-sister-in-law. She said that mine "looked funny." She showed me the easy way to use two whole wraps instead of rolling or folding the rice paper. These are low fat, using chicken or turkey breast and olive oil for cooking. My son who likes spicy foods prefers the Bom Bom chili oil in his wontons. My husband likes his plain. My godson loves the spicier version. A double batch is lucky to last a whole 24 hours. I made a batch of these for an outdoor wedding that was running late. The children at the wedding ate them all by the handful before the reception started.

Ingredients (makes approximately 4 dozen)
2 packages rice paper wonton wraps
1 lb ground turkey breast
6 green onions, finely chopped
1 tsp garlic salt
Pepper to flavor
1 quart olive oil
2 raw eggs
2 tbsp chili oil (optional for a mildly spicy kick)

Directions: Put the olive oil into a 2-quart saucepan and heat on medium, level 4 or lower on an electric stove. Crack two raw eggs in a bowl for rice paper sealant and set aside.

While oil is heating up, mix remaining ingredients in a large bowl. I use a large serving fork to cut the ingredients well into the ground meat. For the spicier version , add 1 tbsp of chili oil or dried red chilis to the mix.

Put 1 regular tsp of meat mixture between two rice paper

wraps. Using your fingers, dip into bowl with eggs and apply egg white on one wrap prior to putting both halves together, edge-to-edge, around the filling. Raw egg white is your glue for wontons. Put one raw wonton in pan. When it rises to the top and turns light golden brown, the oil is hot enough. I usually cook 4 wontons at a time. If you make a double batch, use a 4-quart kettle pan to deep fry them. This has room to cook more wontons at one time, because the pan is larger, but it also requires more oil to cover them. Take cooked wontons out of pan with screened sieve or slotted spoon and put on paper towels to drain. Serve warm with soy sauce on the side. Serves 4-6 people.

Hint: Wontons get slightly mushy and chewy if you microwave them.

Boston Clam Chowder

This is the white-sauce variety of clam chowder with potatoes. I don't particularly like the tomato-based chowder. This is a guaranteed sedative on a cold winter's day and is easy to make. I call this "Becky's valium," as it's guaranteed to make everybody calm, happy, and sleepy. The clams I put in it come chopped up in a 2-quart can from a certain store that specializes in large quantity produce sales. If you use smaller cans of clams, it takes way too many and is very expensive. If you have access to fresh clams, knock yourself out shucking those yummies and dicing them up. Parboiling the chopped potatoes first guarantees a smooth chowder that never has hard, uncooked potatoes in it. Parboiling peeled and diced potatoes in a separate 2-quart pan takes about 5 minutes once the water boils.

Ingredients:

2 lb fresh or saltwater clams, diced and rinsed or 240 mL can with clam juice in it

3-4 cups clam juice (if clams are canned, drain and save the clam juice in a bowl or measuring cup before you rinse them off)

1 large white onion, diced

3 pieces thick bacon or 5 pieces thin bacon, diced

1 tsp black pepper

1 tsp garlic salt

2 bay leaves

1 tsp ground sage

4 regular-sized potatoes, peeled, diced, and parboiled

¾-1 cup flour

2 cups milk

Directions: While the diced potatoes are getting ready to boil in water, start your base (roux). Using a large 6-quart kettle, add the diced bacon, frying it slowly until it is crispy. Add the white onion and fry it until tender in the same large kettle. Take the flour and stir in with the bacon, grease, and onion, adding a little flour at a time, until it stirs like a thick gravy. This is your roux (base).Your potatoes should be boiling by now. If they are not ready (parboiled means slightly crunchy but not hard), add your clam juice that has been drained. If you are using fresh clams, use 3 cups of the potato water and stir into the gravy. Add remaining ingredients and spices once the pot starts to boil on medium-low heat. Cook for 2 hours on medium-low heat. Serves 8 people.

Chicken Satay Kabobs

This is a recipe that you can prepare by marinating the chicken breasts the night before and the day you plan to make it, cooking it on the grill or under the broiler when you come home from work. It is quick and tasty. Kabob bamboo sticks usually come in a pack of 50 or more. You can find them in Asian or Arabian supermarkets even cheaper. I once bought 100 bamboo kabob sticks for $1.50.

Ingredients:
2 lbs skinless chicken breasts, thawed
1 [16 oz] bottle Italian salad dressing
2 tbsp yellow dried curry
¼ tsp dried ginger spice
1 large onion
½ tsp garlic salt
8 bamboo kabob sticks

Directions: Cut chicken breasts up in long slices ½ inch thick. Cut the strips into 2-inch bites. Put chunks of chicken in a casserole or medium bowl. Cover with curry, the whole bottle of Italian salad dressing, garlic salt, and ginger. Stir and let chicken marinate in the refrigerator overnight.

On the next day, cut up large onion into chunks. Pierce chicken longwise and onion chunks onto a kabob until they are at least half full, or half a stick. Sticks will burn a little on the grill, so I usually put the kabobs on foil to prevent the sticks from burning. You can also put them on a cookie sheet and cook them under a broiler, turning them every 10 minutes. If you like to dip the satay kabobs, peanut sauce is the traditional spicy sauce. You can use barbecue sauce, or ranch dressing if you do not like spicy. Makes 4 large or 8 small kabobs. Serves 4-6 people.

Chinese Refried Rice

This is a quick and delicious Chinese favorite. Most of your time is spent preparing the vegetables. Chinese restaurants do not throw out their leftover rice. They use it for egg foo yung and this dish in particular. You can do the same thing with leftover rice in this recipe. You can add one pound of cubed chicken or shrimp if you like. I use a nonstick skillet, which is easier to clean as the rice gets pretty sticky and has to cook longer. This is the vegetarian version that has only eggs and vegetables in it. If you don't have a lot of time when you make this, you can "pre-freeze" the vegetables and cook them frozen. See Cooking Terms and Tips chapter.

Ingredients:
1 whole onion, diced
1 red pepper, diced
1 green pepper, diced
1 cup shredded carrots (you can buy them that way; so much easier)
1 cup raw rice
2 tsp olive oil
2 cups water
3 raw eggs, scrambled
3 tbsp soy sauce

Directions: Start water in a 1-quart saucepan on high to boil. When it is boiling, turn heat down, and add rice. Cover and let cook on simmer or low heat for 20 minutes. Add onion and vegetables with oil in a large nonstick skillet or wok, sprayed with nonstick cooking spray. Fry vegetables on medium heat for 10 minutes in the skillet. Add cooked rice and soy sauce; scramble the eggs with a fork and add to rice. Stir until rice and egg are well cooked. Keep stirring for 40-45 minutes until the rice is dried out and not sticky. Add more soy sauce after serving if you prefer. Serves 4-6 people.

Crunchy Southern Fried Chicken

The secret to making chicken crunchy is in the batter. My grandma also added that if you want your chicken and fish cooked quickly, it needs to swim in oil. The oil I use is usually canola or olive oil and should be at least 2 inches deep. If you make it in a pan, I use a 4-quart kettle, so the oil doesn't splash all over the stove surface. Before I cook the chicken, I use some batter to make deep fried onion rings. Children will always eat onion rings, French fries, and fried chicken because they like the crunch.

Ingredients:
5 cups cooking oil
1 thawed whole chicken or 3 lbs of chicken parts, cut up

Batter Ingredients:
1 egg
1 cup cornstarch
1 cup flour
1 tsp ground pepper
1 ½ cups water
½ tsp salt or 1 tsp complete seasoning for chicken

Directions: Preheat the oil on medium high. Mix all batter ingredients with a whisk or blender and add spices. The batter should be heavy gravy thickness and may need more water if you use too much corn starch. The corn starch is what makes it crunchy. Dip the pieces in the batter until fully covered and drop into hot oil, using tongs. Put the pieces in a single layer in the pan of oil, so it does not stick together. Let cook on medium high until it is golden brown all over and thoroughly cooked. Take chicken out of the oil with tongs and put on paper towels to absorb any excess grease. Serves 4-6 people.

Double Chocolate Chip Cookies

These are one of my family's favorites. They are a little different than regular chip cookies, because they have both dark chocolate and white chocolate chips. They were one of my youngest son's favorites when he was overseas in the military. I tried this recipe with macadamia nuts, but they must be gold-plated, as they are very expensive. The white chocolate gives the cookies a more vanilla taste and accentuates the dark chocolate. I usually have to make a double batch of these, too.

Ingredients:
3 cups white flour
1 ½ cups brown sugar
1 cup white sugar
1 tsp vanilla
1 ½ cups vegetable shortening or 1 cup softened butter
1 tsp baking soda
1 [12 oz] bag semi-sweet or regular chocolate chips
1 [12 oz] bag white chocolate chips
2 eggs

Directions: Preheat oven to 350 degrees Fahrenheit. Mix eggs, baking soda, brown sugar, white sugar, shortening, and vanilla in mixer bowl. Add chocolate and white chocolate chips. Lastly, mix flour in with ingredients, one cup at a time, and stir well. Use 1 tablespoon of cookie dough for each cookie, and place 1 inch apart on ungreased cookie sheet. Bake for 10 minutes or until slightly golden brown. My husband likes them crunchy and I like mine a little chewier, about 8 minutes. Remove from cookie sheet with spatula, and place on wax paper to cool. Makes 10 dozen cookies. At 10 minutes per batch baking time plus mixing ingredients, this recipe takes almost 2 hours.

Empanadas – Caribbean Meat Pies

Empanadas are little meat pies that are found in most countries around the world. I have tried Basque, Caribbean, and Central American Empanadas (which are made with corn maize). My favorite ones were from Africa. The mixture for the centers can be pork, smoked meat, chicken, pineapple, sweet corn, or beef. Use whatever you have left over from a big meal. The seasonings can range from spicy and garlicky to bland and mild. I make mine with flour, as the maize is more difficult to handle. I bake them as pastries, but you can deep fry them as well. This is another good recipe for packing lunches. There is a bakery in Nevada that specializes in Basque meat pies, and the miners buy them for work, breakfast, and lunch.

Center Pie Ingredients:
1 lb meat, diced
1 tsp salt
1 tbsp your favorite seasoning (I use sage and garlic salt for chicken, and for pork I use tomato salsa)
1 onion, diced
2 tbsp olive oil
1 tomato, diced
2 egg whites

Directions: First prepare your dough and roll it out thin on a floured surface (see Pizza Dough recipe in this section).
You will need to roll it on a floured top of a large surface. Mix all of the above ingredients in a 1- to 2-quart saucepan, except for the egg whites, which you will use to seal the pastry. In the medium saucepan, cook the meat mixture over medium or low heat until the meat is tender. While meat is cooking, you

can prepare the flour dough. It does not need to rise. Using a bowl, put the bowl on top of the rolled-out dough, and cut around it to make a perfect circle. Using a spatula, take the circle of dough off of the floured counter surface, and place two tablespoons of the meat mixture on the center of the circle. Use a slotted spoon so you do not get too much fluid with it or your pies will come out soggy. Fold the edges of the dough circle over to meet, and flange the sides using your thumb and two fingers, so it looks like a pie crust. Using the egg white with a basting brush or your fingers, cover the edges so they do not pop open. Repeat the above until you are out of dough or mixture. Put on a large cookie sheet after spraying it with nonstick cooking spray. Bake at 375-400 degrees Fahrenheit for 30-35 minutes, or until the crust is golden brown. I have found that every oven heats differently. The empanadas should be crispy on the edges. Makes 5-6, 5-inch meat pies, or 12, 3-inch pies if you use a smaller bowl to cut your dough.

Greek Lamb

This is my favorite lamb recipe and is an international recipe from the Mediterranean. If it is made right, it will fall off of the bone. I've found that lamb is an acquired taste, but if you use the herbs and spices and cook it correctly, it can taste like veal. To introduce a new dish to your kids, you might have to disguise it with herbs and spices. Most children do not like the red wine version. You can make this with red wine and onions like the traditional osso buco, or you can use lamb shoulder or chops, which are cheaper cuts. Osso buco was actually named after the cut of lamb shank. The secret to cooking lamb is using the correct herbs. I learned this in Istanbul. If you make it right, it has similar flavor, is more pungent, and has the tender texture of beef. I love this with a little tzatziki salad.

Ingredients:
1 whole lamb shank or 6 lbs lamb shoulder, bone included
Mesquite or steak rub, enough to lightly sprinkle all surfaces of the meat
1 tsp thyme
½ tsp finely ground sage
½ tsp garlic salt
1 tsp fresh ground pepper
2 bay leaves
2 large onions, sliced
2 cups red wine (optional)

Note: If you use a lamb shank and want traditional osso buco, use the two cups of red wine, pouring it over the spiced shank before cooking and covering with sliced raw onions.

Directions: Prepare your lamb by thawing it and applying about 2 or 3 teaspoons of meat or barbecue rub of your choice. You need to rub this on evenly to seal in the juices. Preheat oven on 180 degrees Fahrenheit. The lower temperature takes longer to cook but allows the meat enzymes to tenderize the meat (this occurs at any temperature below 200 degrees Fahrenheit). After applying meat rub, sprinkle with thyme, ground pepper, sage, and garlic salt evenly on all sides. After you have coated it with spices, cover with sliced onions, and put in a broiler pan or covered casserole dish and cook for 2 hours per pound. If you have a whole lamb shank (about 8 pounds), you can do this while you are sleeping. Most electric and some propane ovens turn themselves off after 12 hours. Recipe feeds 6 people if you use a lamb shoulder. If you have a whole shank, it depends on how large the shank is, but it should feed 8 or more people if it is an adult 8- to 10-pound lamb shank. Serve with fresh tabouli and a Greek salad with a little tzatziki for a truly international meal. See Chapter One on 30-minute Recipes for tabouli. See International Salads chapter for tzatziki and Greek salad.

Homemade Chicken Pot Pie

This is an old-time favorite and is easy to make. If you don't have the time to make the crust, you can use pre-made pie crusts found in the freezer section of the grocery store. It is a good way to use leftover meats, and my favorite is chicken breasts. This recipe can be used with other types of meat, like kidney pie, an Irish novelty. This is another American and European favorite that is guaranteed to satisfy and put everyone to sleep.

Ingredients:
2 lbs chicken breasts, cubed (about 2 large breasts)
2 large fresh carrots, cubed
1 cup chopped up celery (leaves included)
3-4 medium potatoes, washed and cubed
1 whole large onion, diced
¼ cup flour
2 tsp garlic salt
1 tsp ground pepper
1 tsp sage
1 bay leaf, whole
2 whole pie crusts, thawed

Directions: Preheat oven to 400 degrees. Lay the thawed pre-made pie crust out flat and fit into a round casserole dish or large glass pie pan that is sprayed with nonstick cooking spray. A 9-inch deep-dish pie pan is good. Poke holes in the bottom of the crust with a fork and bake for 15 minutes, until the bottom is brown. Remove from oven.

Take the chicken and cut it up into ½ inch cubes. While the bottom crust is baking, cook the chicken chunks first, until browned, and add remaining ingredients (except the flour) with 1 cup of water. Cover and let stew on medium heat. Stir occasionally. When carrots are parboiled but not hard, add the flour a little at a time to thicken the sauce. This takes about 15 minutes and makes your roux. Pour the thickened stew into the cooled, baked bottom pie crust up to the top, but not over the very edge of the crust. Put the other thawed pie crust on top and flange the top crust to the edge of the pan, joining the other crust. Poke holes in the crust with a fork or sharp knife so it does not crack while baking. Set the pie pan on top of a cookie sheet in case it boils over. This will keep you from cleaning the oven later. Put pie dish or casserole dish in the oven on 400 degrees Fahrenheit for 30 minutes or until the top is brown. Serves 6 people.

Homemade Pie Crust Recipe

I only use this when I am in a part of the world where they do not have the frozen pre-made pie crusts, which is frequently. I have not yet met a child or a husband who does not like homemade pies. I use a potato masher to cut the shortening into the flour, which is much faster than using a fork. My grandmother taught me that. She was a great baker. My grandma and grandpa lived close to a railroad track in Wisconsin. She said that during the Great Depression, she would make two pies, and put one on the outside porch window. The pie would disappear, but they never had anything stolen. A valuable lesson in helping the poor and destitute with limited resources.

Ingredients:
1 tsp salt
2 ½ cups flour
½ cup water
¾ cup whipped or creamed vegetable shortening

Directions: Put salt, vegetable shortening, and flour into a medium-sized mixing bowl. Using a pastry cutter or potato masher, cut the shortening into the dough until it is granular without large lumps. Add water and mix into a large dough ball. Take one half of the dough and put on a floured board or surface and roll it out to 1-2 mm thickness with a rolling pin. Cut to size with a sharp knife and use as a flat crust. To keep dough from sticking, first flour your board or surface and your rolling pin. If the dough sticks, turn the floured side up, and roll it with a little more flour. Makes 2 large 10-inch pie crusts.

Homemade Tortilla Chips

This is one of my favorite local foods that I learned to make in Cuernavaca, Mexico. It is healthier than the chips bought over the counter and you can add just a little salt or flavors like chili powder after they are fried. For a $3 pack of 20-30 corn tortillas, you can both save money and still give your children something good for their lunches or for bean dip with a football game. Corn tortillas that are dried out too much for tacos work just fine for these chips. How do you know if your tortillas are old? If you fold them and they break or fall apart, they are old. These tortilla chips are more flavorful and healthier than the salt-loaded ones you can buy at the store. I use olive oil, which keeps them from getting stale or soggy if you don't eat them right away. I have tried other vegetable oils, but their shelf life is much shorter with other types of oil. This is a true Mexican-American classic.

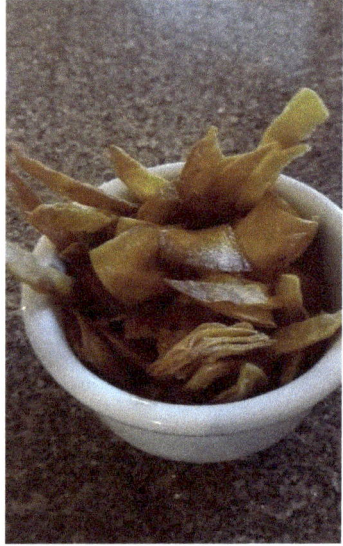

Ingredients:
20 corn tortillas [1 packet]
3 cups olive oil
Salt to taste after the chips are done
Chili powder or other flavored popcorn spices (if you wish a different taste)

Directions: Heat olive oil in the largest skillet that you have on medium-high heat. Cut tortillas into 4 pieces. I use a large chef's knife if they are old, and stack 4-6 tortillas at a time to quarter them. It is faster. Throw quartered tortilla pieces in one layer in hot oil. When they are golden brown around the edges, turn them over with either tongs or a spatula. I use tongs because less oil is wasted when taking them out of the pan. Line a large bowl with paper towels to absorb excess grease. Take chips out of the oil when they are golden brown on both sides and lay in a bowl. Sprinkle with seasoning and salt while they are still warm. Makes 100 healthy, crispy, corn chips, or two large mixing bowls full.

Indian Chicken Tandoori

This is probably my favorite Indian food from the East. Kids like it because even though the yogurt does not have sugar, it gives it a little sweet barbecued flavor. We made this for a fishing club one time and could not get it cooked fast enough for that group. It is simple to make if you have the time to marinate the chicken long enough. In India, they leave the chicken or lamb in large clay pots overnight. This is a faster version; you can put the yogurt and chicken mixture in a casserole dish with skinless chicken and cook at 200 degrees Fahrenheit for one hour. It will absorb more of the flavor, but the chicken still needs to be grilled. An Indian tandoori oven is over 600 degrees Fahrenheit and an outside grill usually only gets up to 500 degrees Fahrenheit. Red curry is the standard for the mixture, but be careful. There are over 300 types of curry, and some are super hot. You want the milder version for the tandoori. I used some biryani curry once and had to rinse the sauce off the chicken so we could eat it, as it was too hot. The yogurt adds the sweetness and you need a hot grill to cook it on once it has marinated. This is usually served with mango or mint chutney. When we went to Singapore, we took the train to the Indian district called Little India just so we could taste the cuisine, and I came back with a bunch of different spices in my suitcase. The underground train system there is amazing, and the flavors are too.

Ingredients:
3 lbs raw chicken, thawed and cut up (any cut will do)
½ cup vegetable or olive oil
1 quart non-flavored yogurt
3 tbsp red curry
1 tbsp coriander

2 tsp salt

3 large onions, sliced

Directions: Wash chicken and pull the skin off. Add yogurt, spices, and skinned chicken to an 8"x10" casserole dish and stir well. Put the sliced onions aside until you are ready to grill them. Put the raw chicken in the mixture and make sure it is well covered. Put in the oven on 200 degrees Fahrenheit for one half hour. Turn chicken over and cook again for 30 minutes. When it is done, the chicken should be dark pink in color. At this stage, you can keep it in the refrigerator until ready to barbecue. Spray the grill with nonstick cooking oil and put the chicken and sliced onions on a sheet of aluminum foil. Fire up the grill to 500 degrees or prepare very hot coals if you do not have a thermometer. Spray foil first with nonstick cooking spray or it will stick because of the yogurt and lack of fat. Cook until the chicken is done all the way through. To grill, put chicken on a hot grill, cover, turn every 5 minutes, and cook until it is well done. It may burn a little on the edges because of the yogurt, but that is expected. Serve with sliced cucumbers, mint chutney, and rice for a genuine Indian meal. Serves 4-6 people, depending on the size of the chicken.

Irish Beef Stew

This is usually made in the winter when you need to get rid of a few old things in the refrigerator or, traditionally, from the root cellar. It is healthy, hearty, and satisfying. For beef, I use steak or any kind of leftover cooked beef in the refrigerator. You cannot make a small batch of this if you are using leftovers; it must be a big pot. This is another dish that warms the stomach and makes children sleepy.

For working parents, this is a good dish to make in the crock pot while you are at work. A hearty meal will be ready to eat when you come home. But with any stew, it takes longer than 30 minutes. I use the whole top of a celery stalk that nobody eats anyway. I keep celery tops in the freezer just for soups and stews (see Cooking Tips). It thickens the broth and you do not need celery salt. It mellows out the flavor and acts as a thickening agent. If you have a carrot or two that is going soft or a couple old potatoes, this is the perfect recipe for using veggies when they are past their prime.

Ingredients:
2 lbs beef, chopped or cubed
3-4 potatoes, washed and chopped
3 large carrots, chopped and cubed
2 cups celery tops, completely diced with leaves
1 medium onion, diced
2 bay leaves
1 tsp ground black pepper
1 cup chopped fresh parsley
1 tsp salt
1 tsp ground sage
1 tbsp crushed garlic
½ cup flour to make the broth (roux) base

3 tbsp olive oil

4 cups water

Directions: Take the cubed beef and fry it in olive oil in a large skillet, adding the garlic, salt, sage, and pepper for flavoring. Once the meat is browned slightly, sprinkle the flour in the broth, and stir into a gravy. Add water if needed so it doesn't lump while stirring. Put the meat, oil, and garlic gravy into a large crock pot or 4-quart kettle and add remaining ingredients, including the water. Stir all ingredients together. Cook until the meat and vegetables are tender, but not mushy. In a crock pot on low, this takes about 8 hours. This dish is especially good with a little fresh bread. In a 4-quart kettle or saucepan, it takes 3-4 hours on low heat. Serves 6-8 people.

Lamb Vindaloo

An Indian dish made with tomato gravy, this can be made very spicy and hot or not spicy at all, depending on which type of red curry that you use. Great for leftover lamb shank or kabob. My son apparently tried this in Afghanistan while he was in the Army, and said it was very good. The other guys were amazed that he could eat the local foods without mishap—another good reason to feed your children something different so that they get used to and like different tastes when they get older. In certain countries, like those in Central America, lamb is difficult to find, so you can substitute a pound of cubed chicken to make Chicken Vindaloo.

Ingredients:
1 lb lamb, cubed
1 [16 oz] can tomato sauce
1 cup peas, frozen, fresh, or canned
1 cup potatoes, cubed and parboiled
½ cup carrots, diced
1 tsp garlic salt (this takes the bitterness out of the tomato sauce)
½ tsp red curry
¼ tsp pepper
½ tsp coriander
2 tbsp olive oil

Directions: Brown the cubed lamb in olive oil over medium heat and add remaining ingredients once the meat is cooked. Stir and cook over low heat until carrots are tender. Serve over white rice. Serves 4-6 people.

Mexican Posole

This is a Mexican traditional soup and, like salsa, is one of my taste tests for a new restaurant. One of my teachers in Mexico said this should be the national soup of Mexico. It is not that spicy and also great for football parties. It is a great dish for leftover meats, and you can also add shrimp if you like. It is the equivalent of Mexican stew and there are recipe variations, depending on the type of chilis grown in the local area. If a good restaurant serves posole, it should be full of flavor and not just spices that burn your tongue off.

Ingredients:
1 [16 oz] can hominy, drained and rinsed
1 large onion, diced
1 cup fresh cilantro, chopped
4 cups chicken broth
1 cup chicken, diced
1 cup lean beef, cut in 1-inch chunks
1 cup ham, diced
1 [8 oz] can tomato sauce
1 large tomato, diced
1 tsp garlic salt
½ cup salsa (of preference)
Ground pepper to taste
1 cup sour cream (for topping)

Directions: Make and heat chicken broth in 4-quart saucepan. You can use leftover, already cooked meat. Chop meat up and add to broth. Add remaining ingredients, except for sour cream, and let cook for 4 hours on medium low. Serve with garnish of sour cream and fresh cilantro on top. Serve with lime slices to give it a spicier flavor. Serves 8 people.

Mikey's Perfect Lasagna

The perfect lasagna is a work of love and this is my husband's recipe. Any Italian will tell you that the sauce needs at least 24 hours to cook out the acidity, or "to age." I use a crock pot, which is much easier. This lasagna is better than any I have had in any American Italian restaurant, except maybe in Italy or New York. We use a glass casserole dish, 8"x13". This makes the cheesy cleanup a whole lot easier. Since the sauce has to cook in a crock pot for 24 hours, I call this a "work of love" recipe. The nice part is that you don't really have to watch it, just stir it once in a while.

Ingredients:
1 ½ lbs hamburger or Italian spicy sausage
2 [16 oz] cans tomato sauce
½ cup garlic, chopped or crushed
½-1 cup powdered Parmesan cheese (for the meat sauce)
1 tbsp dried basil, or 1 cup of fresh basil, chopped
1 tsp dried oregano
2 qt low-fat cottage cheese or ricotta
2 eggs
1 tsp salt
2 boxes lasagna noodles [2 lbs]
½ lb mozzarella cheese, shredded
½ lb provolone cheese, shredded

Directions: Chop up and brown hamburger or Italian sausage in a large frying pan. Sprinkle with pepper if desired. Mix cooked hamburger or sausage with tomato sauce, garlic, Parmesan cheese, basil, oregano, and salt in a large crock pot, and leave on simmer for 24 hours, stirring occasionally. If sauce needs thickening, add another ½ cup of Parmesan cheese, and stir well until melted and thicker. After sauce has cooked in the crock pot for 24 hours, boil water and add lasagna noodles. Cook for 10 minutes or until the pasta is "al dente," which means you can poke a hole in it easily, but it still has some toughness to it. Nobody wants soggy noodles.

Mix 2 quarts of cottage cheese filling (or ricotta) with 2 well beaten eggs and ½ pound of shredded provolone. This makes it more consistent and helps it stick to the noodles better. Spray the casserole dish with nonstick cooking spray. Layer with three full lasagna noodles, longways on the bottom. If your casserole dish is bigger, make one layer on the bottom. Add a layer of meat sauce about 1 cm or ½ inch thick on the noodles with a large wooden spoon or spatula. Add one thin layer of ricotta, egg, and provolone cheese mixture on top of the meat sauce layer. Repeat the layer steps three times. Spread the remaining meat sauce on the top and sprinkle either another cup of Parmesan or Parmesan and mozzarella on the very top of the casserole. Cook at 350 degrees Fahrenheit for one hour or until the top and edges are well done, but not burnt. Serves 8 people.

Perfect Beef Brisket

This is a beautiful brisket and it took me many years to perfect this dish. If you want, you can leave it on low heat in the oven overnight and have delicious brisket perfectly tender in the morning. It is great for sandwiches or the traditional St. Patrick's Day dinner. The secret is in the spices and the slow cooking at low heat. The low temperature lets the meat use all its natural enzymes so that it is tender enough to cut with a fork. I guarantee there will be no uneaten leftovers.

Ingredients:
2 Tbsp. of Montreal steak seasoning rub
1 tsp of garlic salt
1 large beef brisket
1 large roasting pan with a cover

Directions: Preheat oven to 180 degrees Fahrenheit. Wash the brisket and cut the large amounts of excess fat off it. Rub the Montreal steak seasoning, the garlic salt, and the seasoning packet from the package on the top and side of the brisket. Put the fatty side down in the large roasting pan. Put in the oven for 6 hours at 180 °F. Uncover and let cool. Serves 6 people.

Not Papa's Tacos

This is a slight Baja twist to the usual boring beef tacos with a little of Cabo or surf and turf flare. This is the best recipe I have come across in 30 years of traveling to Mexico. I took my kids with me once for a fishing tournament. We watched the chef cook the tacos at the little cabana on the beach. My oldest son ate these tacos like he had a hollow leg.

I prefer these tacos in warm corn tortillas, but you can use pre-made taco shells to save time. You can warm the tortillas in the microwave for one minute with a warm towel and they will be perfect. I called these "not papa's" tacos because my father is allergic to shrimp. He cannot eat them, much to his dismay. If you or your children have shellfish allergies, leave the shrimp out of the recipe. However, shrimp is a Cabo San Lucas staple and makes these tacos even more delicious.

Ingredients:
1 cup fresh shrimp without tails, washed, peeled, and chopped
1 onion, finely diced
1 cup beef, diced (steak or roast leftovers are perfect)
3 slices bacon, chopped in ¼ inch pieces
1 cup tomato sauce
½ cup red salsa of choice
¼ tsp salt
2 tbsp olive oil
12 small corn tortillas
Fresh cilantro for garnish

Directions: This is the easiest, shortest way to warm soft taco shells: wrap tortillas in a clean wet kitchen towel and put in the microwave on high for 45-60 seconds.

Taco Mix Directions: Put diced bacon in large frying pan and cook until brown and crispy. Then add chopped beef and chopped shrimp and onion, and fry in olive oil with the cooked bacon. Add salsa, salt, and tomato sauce. The bacon gives the meat a smoked chipotle taste. Cover and cook on low-medium heat for one hour, until beef is tenderized. Drain off excess juice and fat. Serve in warm taco shells and garnish with cilantro. Serves 4-6 people.

Pizza Dough

I use this same dough recipe for pizza and empanadas (Caribbean and Central American meat pies). It is simple, but not included in my 30-minute recipes because it takes about 30 minutes to rise. If you are at high altitude, it may take longer. This dough will keep well in a baggy in the refrigerator for two or three days, and then you can use it when needed. All kids love pizza. I have tried the recipe on the yeast package, but it does not have enough oil to keep it from sticking or stretching. This is a great dough for empanadas or little meat pies, which can be found in this chapter as well.

Ingredients:
1 package dry yeast or 2 ½ tbsp dry yeast
3 cups flour
1 tsp sugar
1 tsp salt
1 cup warm water
1/3 cup olive oil

Directions: Prepare your yeast first and while it blooms, you can start the flour mixture. The perfect temperature for yeast is 90 to 100 degrees, which is warm water. Over that temperature, it can kill the yeast. Add one package of dry yeast and 1 tsp of sugar to 1 cup of warm water. The sugar helps it work faster. Set aside and let it bloom.

In a large bowl, put your flour and salt in first; make an indentation in the center, and add the oil without stirring. Now your yeast should have a foamy top. If the top is foamy, your yeast is alive. Put the yeast and water mixture in the center of the flour with the oil and mix well with a wooden spoon into a large dough ball. Leave in the bowl, covering the top of the dough ball with a little olive oil gently so that the top does not dry out. Cover bowl with a towel and let sit in a warm place for ½ hour. If you like thick crust pizza, leave the dough covered for one hour or until it doubles. Spray a large pizza pan or cookie sheet with nonstick spray. Once the dough has risen, using your hands or a heavy rolling pin, stretch it to the size you want on a floured surface, and put on a large cookie sheet or pizza pan. If it is sticky from the oil, add a little more flour until it is manageable. Bake with toppings of your choice at 425 degrees Fahrenheit for 15 minutes or until crust is brown. Makes one 18-inch pizza or two 9-inch pizzas. Serves 8 people. If you only need one 9-inch pizza, this dough can be used later if you refrigerate it in a storage baggie.

Real Italian Meatballs

This is a traditional recipe, and I used to grow my own basil in a pot in the winter. If you live in an apartment, basil grows great in a hanging pot. In the South where it does not freeze, it grows year-round. Both of my sons and husband can eat these by the pound, so when I cook for my grown kids, I usually need a double batch. It is the herbs and spices that make the meatballs and gives a whole new flavor to hamburger.

You can freeze these meatballs for up to two months. Then all you need to do is thaw them for pasta or sandwiches and add the sauce. If you don't have time to fry the meatballs, you can leave the whole batch together when all the ingredients are mixed and make a meatloaf with the same savory flavors. The only advantage of using Italian breadcrumbs instead of crushed saltine crackers is that Italian breadcrumbs already have the salt, spices, and oregano in them. I also like to use 1 pound of spicy Italian sausage instead of 2 pounds of hamburger, but since the sausage has more fat, your meatballs will lose weight and size when they cook. Your meatballs may lose weight, but your kids and husband won't. After I've made a batch, my husband checks the refrigerator first and then the freezer.

Ingredients:
2 lbs ground beef
1 cup Italian breadcrumbs (from a box) or 1½ cups cracker crumbs
1 whole large onion, diced
3 eggs
2 cups fresh (not dried) basil, chopped
1 can black olives, chopped and diced (optional)
2 cups olive oil for frying
2 tbsp garlic, minced
¼ tsp black pepper
1 tsp garlic salt
¼ tsp dried oregano

Directions: Heat oil in large frying pan, while mixing all other ingredients in a large bowl. Roll mixture in your hands into 3-inch round meatballs and place in frying pan gently. Turn over with a large spoon or tongs until dark brown all over and put on paper towels to absorb excess oil when done. Meatballs are done when they are not pink in the middle, and brown and crispy on the outside. Add to Italian prepared sauce of choice. Can serve with spaghetti, other pastas, or on bread for a meatball sandwich. Garnish with Parmesan cheese if you like. Freeze leftover meatballs without the sauce in a one-gallon freezer bag and use as needed. Makes 12-18 meatballs.

Spanakopitas

A dish that every Greek and most Mediterranean families have made, there are different twists and recipes on each island for spanakopita. These are the fastest and tastiest that I have made. You can serve spinach to a finnicky eater, disguised by pastry dough and low-fat or ricotta cheese, and they will eat them without complaint. Phyllo dough sheets are found in the frozen pastry section of the supermarket, along with premade pie crusts. You will need a butter basting brush, which can be found in most department stores. A small, unused 2-inch paint brush will also work. These are the traditional spanakopita flavor without tomatoes or other additives.

Ingredients:
2 raw eggs
1 quart nonfat ricotta or cottage cheese
2 tsp garlic salt
¼ tsp ground pepper
2 lbs frozen spinach, chopped
1 box phyllo dough sheets, thawed
1 stick melted butter

Directions: Preheat oven to 375 degrees Fahrenheit. Beat the eggs. Mix eggs, nonfat cheese, frozen spinach, and spices in a 2-quart saucepan and heat on medium-low while stirring. Set aside when the mixture is hot. Drain any liquid off the mixture.

While spinach cheese mixture is cooling, unroll the phyllo dough. Take phyllo dough out of package and unroll gently to check if it is completely thawed. There is a wax paper cover that is rolled up with the dough to keep it from sticking together. Remove wax paper cover. Put all large sheets together flatly on a dry cutting board or surface, and cut all pieces in quarters at one time, using a sharp chef's knife. Spray a large cookie sheet with nonstick cooking spray. Take one of the quarters of the dough, with 4-5 thin sheets at a time. Place on cookie sheet and cover top sheet with basting brush and light coat of melted butter. Do this twice so that your base layer for the pastry pies is at least 10 thin sheets thick. The second layer of butter on top will make the pastry stick when you fold it over. Add 3 tablespoons of spinach filling in the center of the butter-basted dough. Put the spinach mixture in the middle of the square and fold pastry from corner to corner over the filling. Baste the top of the pastry with butter. This ensures a crispy golden top once baked. Fold the edges over each other ½ inch to prevent the center filling from leaking out. You should have a 3"x5" triangular pastry spinach pie. Leave on cookie sheet and repeat procedure until all spinach mixture is used. Bake at 375 degrees Fahrenheit for 30 minutes or until golden brown on the top. Makes 6, 4"x5" pastries

Supa Toscano

This is an Eastern European favorite and a winter staple for those years before the refrigerator was invented. I like making it when the weather starts to chill in the fall. This is another "sleepy-time" dish. The warm soup lulls everyone into relaxation, which is important when mom has to study for a test the next day. Feed kids soup at 6 p.m., and they will be asleep by 8 p.m. It reheats well, too. As most soups sit, even in the refrigerator, the spices get a little more blended and taste better. This soup is made with potatoes and sausage, which is what the Europeans would have left over in the winter. The Italians use Italian parsley, but I like cilantro better. If you have a few potatoes that are going soft and a pound of Italian sausage, this is the perfect winter dish.

Ingredients:
1 cup fresh cilantro, chopped
1 cup fresh basil, chopped
3 large potatoes, diced
1 lb Italian sausage
½ tsp garlic salt
2 cups milk
1 medium onion, diced
¼ tsp fresh ground black pepper to taste
¼ cup olive oil
½ cup flour

Directions: Cover the diced potatoes with water and boil them in a 2-quart saucepan to parboil them—this way, your potatoes are well cooked in the soup and not crunchy. While the potatoes are getting ready to boil, cut up the Italian sausage, then brown in a 4-quart saucepan with the onion and olive oil. Cook sausage until brown. Add the flour while stirring and then add ½ cup of the milk, stirring slowly to make the roux, or base, of the soup. Add remaining ingredients: the rest of the milk, 2 cups of the potato water, parboiled potatoes, salt, pepper, fresh basil, and cilantro. Cook over low to medium heat for 1 hour, stirring occasionally. Serves 6 people.

Sweet Potato Chips

This is nutritious and your kids will love them. If you use fresh yams, they are even sweeter. I got tired of paying $3.25 for 6-8 ounces of healthy chips. You can use fresh apples, but that is a different recipe and apple chips are baked. If you use olive oil, it burns fat, and is healthier. You will need one important piece of cooking equipment. A slicing mandolin is not very expensive and is found at various department stores. I have tried these chips with yucca, but they are tougher, and not as crunchy. A mandolin cuts the chips extra thin and they taste better than store bought. These are great for packing in kids' and adults' lunches. These are high in vitamin C and vitamin D, and do not contain preservatives.

Ingredients:
2 large sweet potatoes or fresh yams
3 cups olive oil
Sea salt for flavoring

Directions: Heat your oil up first on medium-high in the largest frying pan you have. You can use a deep fryer, which is faster, if you have one. On an electric stove, medium-high is 3.5 to a 4 setting. If the olive oil is smoking, the setting is too hot.

Use the mandolin safety grabber to slice the potatoes, to protect your fingers. Slice the potatoes thinly with a mandolin and set aside until the oil is hot. I prefer to slice the potatoes longwise, so they make longer, crunchy, big chips. Then add enough thin-sliced potatoes to cover the bottom of the pan in a single layer, about ½ cup of slices, and cook until golden brown. If you want to add salt, you can add it after or during cooking. Remove chips with a sieve-spoon for deep frying, a long-handled fork, tongs, or strainer, and place on paper towels to absorb any excess oil. To keep these crisp, you need open containers, as a baggy will make them soggy. In my kitchen, they do not last long enough in a bowl to get soggy. Serves 4-6, depending on the size of two yams.

Secret Sauces

Secret Sauces are not so secret. A good chef can eat at a restaurant, then reproduce the same sauces at home, which is quicker and easier, without preservatives. My children had no idea that they were eating homemade sauces. I save the old dressing bottles, wash them out well, and add the homemade sauces to the same bottle. I have gathered a few of the most important basic sauces like cocktail sauce, and will avoid the spicier curry or truffle varieties. I love sharing my sauce secrets with you.

Basic Shrimp Cocktail Sauce

Ingredients:
½ cup catsup
1 tsp creamed horseradish

Directions: Mix catsup with horseradish until it is thoroughly mixed together. Serve with shrimp or kabobs. You can add more horseradish if you like it hotter. Makes ½ cup of dip.

Chipotle Sauce
(for hamburgers or salad dressing)

Chipotle is by tradition a blend of smoked hot peppers. It gives this sauce a little Mexican kick.

Ingredients:
½-1 tsp chipotle ground spice
4 tbsp mayonnaise or fat-free substitute
1 tbsp catsup

Directions: Mix ½ tsp of chipotle spice with mayo and catsup until uniform in color. Taste it first before adding the rest of the spice. Some spices are quite hot, and some are milder depending on the brand. If there is no smoky flavor, and it is not too spicy for you, add the other ½ tsp of chipotle.

Thousand Island Basic Recipe

A traditional sauce for those with a sweet tooth. Used for salads or hamburgers.

Ingredients:
½ cup mayonnaise or fat-free substitute
½ cup catsup
2 tbsp chopped relish or sweet pickles
Salt and pepper to taste

Directions: Mix all ingredients in bowls until uniform in color and consistency. Add salt and flavor until you think it is perfect, a little at a time. Makes 1 cup of dressing.

Granny's Barbecue Sauce

This sauce is for those who are tired of the barbecue sauce falling off of their ribs, chicken, and brisket. This recipe was handed down to me by one of the most special southern cooks that I have ever known, who taught me how to cook southern food while I was a young student in Missouri. My oldest son is now asking me for her recipes, so I think he will like this book. Once again, I use a barbecue sauce bottle or catchup bottle and fill it up with the leftover sauce. This sauce is sweet, sticky, and will not drip off of your meat.

Ingredients:
1 cup molasses
1 cup honey
2 cups catsup
2 tsp liquid smoke

Directions: If you are smoking the meat before cooking, you do not need the liquid smoke, as the flavor will come from the wood chips. If you make your meat in a roasting pan or in the oven, the liquid smoke is necessary. Mix all ingredients together well and pour on top of the meat you are cooking in a thin layer. Spread it out on the meat using a fork or a large spoon. This is enough for two large racks of ribs, front and back, or one whole cut-up chicken. I have used it for venison, but the secret to cooking a tender deer is to cut the thin fascia off of the meat first. If you like barbecued venison, cook it at low heat for a longer period of time, because it is a low-fat meat. If you like it spicy, use a rub on the meat first, or add red peppers or chipotle spice to the mixture. I put the leftover sauce in an empty catsup bottle for those who like it on a little thicker and set it with the meat on the table.

Sweet and Spicy Chinese Sauce for Stir-Fry and Dipping

This is a quick and easy sauce and can be used on any meat. It is the basis for the sauce used in Kung Pao dishes and General Tso's chicken recipes. I like to use rice noodles and a deep fried or broiled meat with this. It is spicier than barbecue sauce, but still sweet. It can also be used alone for dipping egg rolls or wontons.

Ingredients:
1 cup Mae Ploy Thai sweet chili sauce
½ cup soy sauce, low salt if you prefer

Directions: Mix above two ingredients in a saucepan and heat on low heat, add noodles and meat, or just cut fresh vegetables if you prefer and steam for 10 minutes. If used for dipping, chill sauce first and serve in small bowls. Serves 6.

Green Tomato Salsa

This is a great recipe for those of us who have short growing seasons and lots of green tomatoes that do not completely ripen. All you need is a hearty blender and a large pot. I can about a dozen jars of this each year, just enough to last the winter. You can usually find smoked peppers, known as chipotle in a carniceria (butcher shop). You can find canned or dried chipotles in the Latin or Mexican food sections of many supermarkets. The canned ones tend to be much hotter though, so don't add a whole can without tasting it first. This is another good dip for football parties with tortilla chips. If you live in the North or have a sudden cold freeze, this is the perfect salsa for using those tomatoes.

Ingredients:
4-6 whole green tomatoes, sliced in quarters
1 bunch cilantro, chopped finely
3 smoked chipotle jalapeños
1 cup water

Directions: Wash cilantro and tomatoes, then put all ingredients in a large blender. Blend until pureed, pour mixture into a 4-quart pan, and cook on low heat until boiling. Let boil for 5 minutes, and it is ready to can or put in a jar in the refrigerator. I like to serve it with some chopped green onions on top for extra flavor. Makes 2 quarts.

Peruvian Salsa Verde

This is a pungent but not super hot green sauce that is used from Central America to the Andes. In Central America, they call the herb culantro, which is a larger and more pungent plant than the North American cilantro. In Panama, this sauce is called chimichurri. It grows better in the Central and South American mountains, where it is slightly cooler. You can use either type of cilantro.

This sauce is an asset to barbecued meat and also works well as a marinade. For those areas that have tough free-ranged cattle, marinating the meat is a necessity for tenderness. Children do not eat tough meat, and the lime juice in this recipe will tenderize the meat so they can chew it. Otherwise, you will find all the tough pieces cut off and spread around the outside of their plates.

Ingredients:
2 cups or 2 bunches washed cilantro or culantro
1 cup freshly squeezed lime juice
1 tsp garlic salt

Directions: Cut the stems off of the freshly washed cilantro or culantro and put all ingredients into a blender. Blend until pureed and pour into a small bowl. Heat in a small pan until boiling to kill any bacteria, and cool in the refrigerator. If you need this as a marinade for chicken or red meat, you will have to double the recipe.

French Fruit Compote

I use fresh fruit for this recipe, or frozen fruit with the juices drained off. You can use canned fruit, but you just need the juice. Fresh or fresh frozen fruit is healthier and higher in antioxidants. If you have children with ADHD or sugar sensitivity, try using the sativa sugar substitute. It is organic and made from a mint plant.

Fruit compote is a smooth fruit sauce that you can pour over ice cream or pastries for a scrumptious treat. It dresses up a dessert that would be boring. I have used canned peaches, frozen blueberries, and other fruits. Cook the fruit on simmer for 30 minutes, covered, and you can pour the juice off of it. You can add a shot of brandy for flavor if you like, and the alcohol burns off when you boil it. This sauce is yummy with canned peach compote on peach turnovers.

Ingredients:
1 cup unsweetened fresh fruit juice (your favorite flavor)
¼ cup sativa sugar substitute or sugar
¼ cup corn syrup
1 tbsp tapioca powder for thickening

Directions: Spray small saucepan with nonstick cooking spray to make your cleanup easier. Boil fruit juice and all ingredients in a small saucepan on low heat until bubbling gently. Add tapioca and keep on low heat until the tapioca dissolves—it will take about 10 minutes to thicken. The compote should be the consistency of jam preserves. Once tapioca is dissolved, pour over ice cream or pastry. Serves 4 people.

Mexican Red Salsa

This is a smoky version of Mexican salsa that I really like. If you are into canning and have a bumper crop of tomatoes, you can also can this. If you use canned tomatoes, drain them first. This is another good side dip for football parties or sleepovers. The chipotle adds just enough smoke flavor and spice. Be careful of the canned chipotle peppers, which are a lot hotter.

Ingredients:
3 lbs fresh red tomatoes or 1 [16 oz] can whole tomatoes (romas work best)
1 large smoked jalapeno or red chipotle smoked pepper
1 tsp salt
½ tsp black pepper
1 bunch fresh cilantro, washed and chopped

Directions: Put all ingredients in a blender and puree. Serve cold. Makes one quart.

Thanksgiving Cranberry Sauce

This is a really tasty cranberry dish. I refuse to eat cranberries out of a can. My kids were not thrilled about cranberries. Cranberries are a bitter fruit, but if cooked fresh, they are tasty, nutritious, and can even make a good pie or pastry filling. Children will eat this eat this one and leave the canned jelly on the table untouched.

Ingredients:
2 lbs fresh cranberries, washed
1 cup brown sugar or brown sugar substitute
1 tbsp tapioca
¼ tsp cloves
1 tbsp cinnamon
1 orange, peeled and diced

Directions: Put all ingredients in a large 2-quart saucepan, cover on medium-low heat, and let boil, while stirring occasionally to prevent burning. Stir in the tapioca until it is well melted. When it has thickened and the berries are soft, it's done. If you would prefer cranberry jelly, put the sauce into a blender on puree setting, and pour into a bowl. Put in the refrigerator to cool until it gels. Serves 6-8 people.

2-Minute Nacho Cheese Sauce

This is a slightly spicy cheese sauce and it is good on broccoli too. Remember that if you need to disguise your vegetables for the younger kids, remove the garlic chili sauce. Most children do not develop their spicy taste buds until after age 5. This is another good football party or sleepover dip for tortilla chips. This recipe takes two minutes in the microwave and is better than the nacho sauce you buy in the jar.

Ingredients:
8 oz American cheese, shredded or sliced
¼ cup milk
1 tsp Thai garlic chili sauce (comes in a jar already mixed—
leave this out for broccoli or vegetable sauce)

Directions: Put shredded or sliced cheese in a microwaveable jar or bowl, in the microwave on high for one minute. Take out of the microwave and stir in the milk and Thai garlic chili sauce. Put in the microwave for one more minute and stir after the second minute. If it is not melted completely, repeat on microwave for one more minute or less. Some microwaves vary in strength and temperature. Best served warm. You can pour it over nacho chips or serve by itself as a dip. Makes one cup of cheese dip.

Chinese Sweet and Sour Sauce

I use this for sweet and sour stir-fry and for dipping egg rolls. It is not as spicy as my Sweet and Spicy Recipe. I avoid red dyes and preservatives, and this tastes better than store bought brands.

Ingredients:
1 cup pineapple juice
Juice of one lemon
1 cup honey
½ cup soy sauce
1 tbsp fresh ginger, chopped small

Directions: Do not use the lemon juice made from concentrate. It has potassium sorbate as a preservative and your sauce will taste funny. Add all ingredients in small saucepan and bring to a boil to soften the ginger. If used for stir-fry, add meats to this after stir-frying vegetables in a large frying pan. If used for dipping, chill and serve in small bowls.

Raspberry Vinaigrette

This is a delicious and healthy way to dress a salad, and is a component of the Spinach, Walnut, Cranberry salad recipe. It keeps well in a bottle in the refrigerator and has no preservatives. The vinegar is the only preservative.

Ingredients:
2 cups frozen raspberries
1 cup apple vinegar
¼ tsp salt
2 tbsp honey

Directions: Put two cups of frozen raspberries in a 1-quart pan and heat until boiling. Turn heat down. Cook on medium heat for 15 minutes and remove from heat. Put raspberries and apple vinegar in a blender with salt, and frappe. Put in a cruet or measuring cup in the refrigerator to cool.

Quick Desserts

I made most of these for my children and myself, who have finnicky sweet tooths. They are not at all time consuming, and they're easy to make. My grandmother taught me that every child has a sweet tooth, and she used to pack lunches with a piece of cake or brownie. If the kids didn't like the sandwich, they would always eat the dessert.

Banana Split Brownies

This is an easy but very rich dessert for those in your family who are ice cream or chocolate addicts. Chocolate has two contrasting effects in different children—it will either make them sleepy or make them hyperactive. The bananas change the taste a lot, so don't use too many. Hopefully, the tryptophan from the bananas will counteract the hyperactivity from the chocolate.

Ingredients:
1 prepackaged brownie mix (use recommended ingredients on the box)
2 large bananas

Directions: Preheat oven to 350 degrees Fahrenheit. Combine brownie mix according to the directions on the box in the same pan as the box instructions suggest. Slice bananas into 1 cm or ¼ inch pieces. Pour one-half of the brownie mixture into the baking pan after spraying with nonstick cooking spray. Layer the bananas on top of the chocolate mixture. Pour remaining brownie mix over the bananas. Cook as directed on the box. Serve with one scoop of ice cream and toppings of choice. Serves 12.

Brown Sugar Frosting

This is a very quick and great topping for a number of cakes and cupcakes. Of course, it is pure sugar, but can be made with sativa brown sugar if you can find it.

Ingredients:
2 ½ cups brown sugar or brown sugar substitute
1 stick [½ cup] unsalted butter

Directions: Spray a 1- or 2-quart saucepan with nonstick spray and add the two ingredients above. Believe me, spraying your pan first will make cleaning later much easier. Stir over medium-low heat until sugar is melted and no longer grainy. This frosting can be made while you are baking a cake. Pour on cake once thickened.

Easy S'mores

This is a timeless recipe that every Girl Scout and Boy Scout will learn if they go camping.

The reason they are usually made at the campfire is that they are messy, sticky, and gooey. The other reason they are made while camping is so if the children get hyperactive from a sugar rush, they have room to run all that energy off. I try to contain the chocolate mess with a foil wrapper and use a toaster oven range to make the same at home. You can pack these in lunches if you use the foil to wrap them. Pick up the package and let your guests open them outside. These are good for outdoor barbecues as well.

Ingredients:
12 graham crackers
1 roll aluminum foil
1 bag marshmallows
2 large chocolate bars [8.6 oz each]

Directions: Cut 6 pieces of foil 6 inches wide. Lay one graham cracker on the foil, two squares of chocolate bar on one graham cracker, followed by 5 or 6 small marshmallows (or 2 large ones), and cover with other graham cracker. Wrap the complete cracker, chocolate, and marshmallow sandwich tightly with foil until all edges are well covered. You can cook these on a grill for 15 minutes each, turning them once with a spatula, or in a toaster oven on 350 degrees Fahrenheit for 15 minutes. Makes 6 s'mores.

French Fruit Parfait

This is a cool dish that you can prepare before you cook a 30-minute meal. It takes less than 30 minutes if you use frozen fresh fruit, which keeps longer. It is super easy and super yummy. My kids have no idea that this was a gourmet recipe. The flavor beats any of those prepackaged lunch puddings. If you are making these for lunches, you can layer the fruit in small Tupperware containers.

Ingredients:
1 container whipped cream topping
1 cup fresh fruit (strawberries, cherries, blueberries—can be frozen)
1 cup sliced bananas (about 2 medium bananas)
 4 [8 oz] glasses

Directions: Put one single layer of sliced bananas in bottom of glasses first. Add 2 tablespoons of whipped cream topping to cover each layer. Put another layer of berries, frozen, or fresh fruit on top of the first layer, and cover with 2 tablespoons of whipped cream topping, then continue layers until glass is almost full. Put one slice or piece of fruit on the top of the last whipped cream layer. You can usually get three layers of fruit in an 8 ounce glass. Put in refrigerator until dessert. If you use frozen fruit, leave them out of the refrigerator so that the fruit thaws. You can use non-dairy whipped topping if you are lactose intolerant. Non-dairy whipped topping is less fattening than whipped cream and freezes well. Serves 4 people.

German Gingerbread Kuchen

This is a holiday recipe that only takes 30 minutes to cook, and makes the whole house smell delightful. It is actually a German cake and traditionally made during the Christmas or Hanukah season.

Ingredients:
2 cups vegetable shortening
1 egg
1 cup dark molasses
1 cup white or brown sugar
2 tbsp ground cinnamon
3 cups flour
3 tsp ground ginger
½ tsp salt
1 tsp baking soda
½ cup sliced almonds

Directions: Preheat oven at 350 degrees Fahrenheit. Put one raw egg, the vegetable shortening, molasses, sugar, salt, baking soda, cinnamon, and ground ginger in a large bowl and stir until thoroughly mixed. Stir in the flour until thoroughly mixed into a stiff batter. Spray a glass or metal 8"x12" pan with nonstick spray. Pour the dough mixture into the pan and spread evenly with a spatula. Sprinkle the sliced almonds on the top with two tablespoons of sugar. Bake at 350 degrees Fahrenheit for 30 minutes. Test with a toothpick or cool knife by sticking it in the middle—if it comes out clean, without batter on it, the center is done. Serve warm or cold. Cut into one or two-inch squares.

French Pastry Tortes

This recipe is easy but requires a pastry brush and melted butter to make the dough stick. I have made pastry layers from scratch before, and it is a very time-consuming procedure. I use pre-frozen, pre-layered phyllo dough, which works just as well, and will surprise everybody in your family as an excellent dessert. If you made the dough yourself, it would take at least an hour just to roll the layers out. You can put any fruit or flavor in the tortes that you like. I have used fresh apples, canned peaches, frozen cherries, and other fillings. Make sure you drain the liquid off the fruit, so the pastries do not get soggy. Also thaw the phyllo dough first at room temperature or store it in the refrigerator until you are ready to use it. If the butter is too fattening, you can use oleo or margarine. It will stick too. If you have children, you might want to make a double batch, because these are super yummy when warm out of the oven.

Ingredients:
1 box phyllo dough (found in the freezer section of the market)
1 stick butter
1 large can pie filling of your choice or 4 cups fresh fruit or frozen fruit of your choice
1 tsp tapioca
1 cup sugar or organic sugar substitute (only if you are using fresh fruit)

Directions: Put fruit in a small saucepan if it is fresh, add sugar, tapioca, and cook down on medium heat until the tapioca is dissolved and the sauce is thickened. If using canned pie filling, you can skip this step. Put butter in a glass bowl and melt in microwave for 30 seconds. You may have to repeat if your butter is really cold. If you leave butter in the microwave too long, it will explode. Preheat oven to 375 degrees Fahrenheit.

Take phyllo dough out of package and unroll gently. If it is completely thawed, you'll see that there is a wax paper cover that is rolled up with the dough to keep it from sticking together. Put large sheets on a dry surface, and cut all pieces in quarters at one time, using a sharp chef's knife. Spray a large cookie sheet with nonstick cooking spray. Take one of the quarters of the dough, with 4-5 thin sheets at a time. Place on cookie sheet and cover top sheet with basting brush and light coat of melted butter. Do this twice so that your base layer for pastry is at least 10 thin sheets thick. The second layer of butter on top will make the pastry stick when you fold it over. Add 2 tablespoons of fruit filling in the center of the butter-basted dough. Put the fruit in the middle of the square and fold pastry from corner to corner over the filling. Baste the top of the pastry with butter. This ensures a crispy golden top once baked. Fold the edges over each other 1/2" to prevent the center filling from leaking out. You should have a 3"x5" triangular pastry.

Leave on cookie sheet and repeat procedure until all dough is used. Sprinkle complete pre-baked pastries with cinnamon. Bake at 375 degrees Fahrenheit for 30 minutes or until golden brown on the top. Makes 6, 4"x5" pastries. A little whipped cream or caramel syrup drizzled on top makes this look like a dessert from a 5-star restaurant.

Puffed Pastry Tarts

This is an elegant but extremely simple recipe for a tour de force dessert.

Ingredients:
6 oz jar raspberry jelly (or your flavor of choice)
2 boxes thawed pastry puffs (usually found in the frozen pie dough section)
Whipped cream in a spray can
Caramel or chocolate sauce

Directions: Preheat oven at 350 degrees Fahrenheit. Cut pastry sheets in 3-inch pieces while folded. Remove any paper from inside the pastry. Put one tablespoon of jelly into 2 of the folds on each cut piece. Spray cookie sheet with nonstick cooking spray. Lay jellied pastry on a nonstick cookie sheet. Leave a little room for the air to circulate around each piece. Bake in the oven 25-30 minutes. Pastries should be puffed up and golden brown. Serve topped with whipped cream and choice of chocolate or caramel sauce. Serves 8-10 people.

Quickest Chocolate-Covered Bananas

I made this dessert by accident because I bought a bunch of small bananas in Central America that were going to rot. You can buy a whole bunch of bananas, not per pound, but for $2 a bunch on the stalk. Unfortunately, there are only so many bananas that you can eat. So, I peeled and froze the rest. The Manzano bananas in Central America are not as large as the Chiriqui bananas you get in the United States, but they are sweeter. To perform this recipe well, you should peel and freeze them first and make this dessert later, when you want to impress somebody.

Ingredients:
1 lb milk chocolate chips or 2 [8 oz] chocolate bars
8 small bananas about 5 inches long each, peeled and frozen
Canned whipped cream
1 shot dark rum

Directions: Chocolate chips work better in this recipe because they melt faster. But in Central America, you cannot always find them. Take the chocolate chips, and/or break up the chocolate bars into smaller chunks. Put in a 2-quart nonstick saucepan, or double boiler, and simmer on lowest heat until chocolate is melted, stirring constantly. Remove from heat. (Note: do not add milk to thin the chocolate, or you will end up with a lump of fudge instead.) If it is still too thick, add a shot of your favorite rum to it. Put a large sheet of wax paper on top of an 8"x12" cookie sheet and spray with nonstick cooking spray. Using tongs, dip each frozen banana into chocolate sauce until it is well covered. Place on wax paper. Repeat for each banana. Put cookie sheet in refrigerator until dessert. Serve bananas whole, one per plate. Spray a row of whipped cream on each serving. Serves 8 people.

International Salads

Some of these salads are American favorites. Some are served in restaurants that specialize in other types of cuisines or just salads. Like most parents, I have one child that likes his green salads, and one child who doesn't. This section includes both, although the green salads are much healthier.

American Potato Salad

This one of my husband's favorite dishes and an American standard for summer picnics. It is quick and easy and makes a large amount for 6-8 people. You can substitute sweet pickles instead of dill pickles if you like a sweeter tang to your salad.

Ingredients:
6 eggs, hard-boiled
6 large potatoes, chopped
up into squares
1 ½ cups mayonnaise
4 green onions, diced
4 small potatoes, cut longwise
1 can sliced black olives
2 medium sliced dill pickles, diced up
2 tsp garlic salt
1 tbsp dried mustard
1 tsp ground black pepper
2 tbsp dried dill

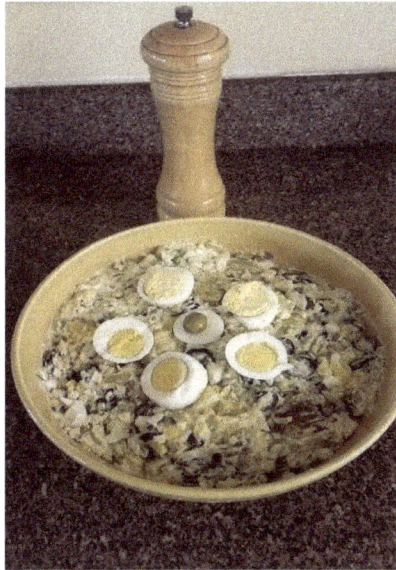

Directions: Boil the potatoes that have been cut up in a 2-quart saucepan with the eggs until potatoes are tender enough to stick a fork in them, but not mushy. Boil the eggs while the cubed potatoes are boiling. It only takes about 30 minutes to parboil the potatoes and hard boil the eggs. Drain both well. Peel the hard-boiled eggs and dice them up. Mix all ingredients in a large bowl for serving. Chill before serving. Serves 6-8 people.

Asian Mandarin Chicken Salad

This is a great dish for leftover grilled chicken breasts. Since my husband only eats the breasts, that is all I buy most of the time, unless we have a big batch of friends over. This is a healthy dish and easy to make.

Ingredients:
2 cans mandarin oranges with the syrup
2-3 lbs chicken breast, thawed or already cooked
1 head lettuce
1 bag dry chow mein wheat noodles
½ cup soy sauce
1 tsp fresh ginger, diced up in small pieces
1 can sliced water chestnuts
Salt and pepper to taste

Directions: Make the sweet sauce first. Put the ginger, soy sauce, and juice from the canned mandarin oranges in a 1-quart saucepan and cook on medium heat, while you are cutting the lettuce and chicken breasts. If the chicken breasts are not cooked yet, cut the skin off, salt and pepper them to taste and cook the chicken 5 inches under the broiler for 15 minutes. When they are done, cut them off of the bone, and slice lengthwise into 1-2 inch strips. Take the sauce off the burner and stir. Add a little pepper to taste and put sauce in a small glass bowl and put in the refrigerator to cool. Make a salad bed of chopped lettuce, then add drained water chestnut slices and 1 cup of dried Chinese chow mein noodles. Mix well, tossing the ingredients together. Put the sliced chicken on the top of the salad, garnish with fresh crunchy noodles, and use the cooled sauce for salad dressing. I like to serve my sauce separately in a cruet or gravy bowl so everyone can use what they want. Serves 4-6 people.

Caribbean Tropical Fruit Salad

I love to make this when the summer fruits are available and fresh. It is healthy, delicious, and cool on a hot summer's day. It is sweet enough to please even the most finnicky eaters. And it is loaded with healthy vitamins and minerals. You can used canned pineapple, but I prefer a fresh ripe one. However, in the northern hemisphere, this can be a challenge. If a pineapple is ripe, when you pull a leaf out of the top easily, it is ready to eat. When I lived in the mainland United States, I used to have to let the pineapple and mangoes set out for a week before they were ripe enough to eat. This salad is even better if you have a couple of ripe kiwis to add.

Ingredients:
3 mangos, ripened (pink and soft to the squeeze)
1 whole pineapple (or 1 [16 oz] can sliced rings)
1 medium ripe papaya (orange—not green)
3 ripe bananas
1 cup shredded coconut

Directions: Peel bananas, mangoes, and papaya, and remove the seeds. To cut a pineapple, remove the top and bottom with a large sharp chef's knife. Then cut the outside peel and little stickers off. Cut the pineapple lengthwise. You can use the center if it is ripe, tasty, and not too tough. Chop up pineapple, mangoes, and papaya into 1-inch squares. Add sliced bananas. Stir in one cup of shredded coconut. Serves 6 people.

Greek Oliues

I love these little jewels of the Mediterranean, but they are pricey at the stores. These are easy to make, and you can also use this recipe for artichoke hearts. I keep these in the refrigerator in a covered bowl and use them as hors d'oeuvres, or on pizza and pasta. They don't spoil and don't need to be cooked. These are so easy to make that I refuse to pay the high prices for a pint of them anymore at the grocery store.

Ingredients:
1 cup vinegar
½ cup minced garlic
1 tsp fresh oregano
1 tsp garlic salt
1 can whole black olives or artichoke hearts

Directions: Put all ingredients into a glass bowl after draining the juice from the olives and/or the artichoke hearts. Cover, and keep in the refrigerator. It takes about two weeks for the olives to turn brown from the pickling.

Greek Salad

Traditional Greek salads have Greek olives in them. See the recipe above if you want to make your own. Otherwise, they can be quite expensive in a deli. Feta goat cheese is the traditional cheese, but shredded mozzarella works just as well if you can't get feta. Feta does not usually trigger lactose-intolerant allergies because it is made from goat's milk. It still contains a little lactose, which is reduced by the fermentation process. Mozzarella has a lot more regular lactose. The Greek olives are what makes the salad.

Ingredients:
1 lb feta cheese
1 lb fresh spinach, without the stems, washed
2 cups Greek olives, drained
1 head iceberg lettuce, chopped
5-6 pickled pepperoncinis, sliced
1 tsp dried basil or ½ cup fresh basil leaves
1 cup shredded mozzarella (for topping)
½ tsp garlic salt

Directions: Break up the feta cheese into small ½-1" chunks. Add fresh washed spinach leaves, chopped up iceberg lettuce, sliced pepperoncinis, and whole Greek olives in a large bowl. Sprinkle with garlic salt and mix salad. Stir well and sprinkle the shredded mozzarella on top for garnish. Serve it with your favorite dressing and fresh ground pepper. Serves 6-8 people.

Egg Salad

Easy and healthy for lunches and sandwiches. Eggs are misunderstood by a lot of people in fear of the cholesterol content. Eggs contain choline, which is a natural food for the brain. Teenagers need more "brain food" like omega-3 acids and protein because their brains are developing faster during their growth spurts. You might think your child is perfect. Wait until they hit age 13. Once their hormones start surging and their brains develop faster, their behavior changes and they become more spontaneous. One egg is only 100 calories. If you want less cholesterol, try this with nonfat mayonnaise made from avocado or soy oil.

Ingredients:
5-6 large hard-boiled eggs
3 green salad onions, chopped
1 cup nonfat mayonnaise
¼ tsp black pepper
½ tsp salt to flavor
1 dash dry mustard

Directions: Chop eggs up into small pieces. Wash and chop up green salad onions. Add all ingredients together and blend well in a 2-quart bowl. Makes 4 regular-sized sandwiches on bread, or you can use one cup of salad served on a lettuce leaf for a more elegant salad. Garnish with a sprig of parsley.

Italian Pasta Salad

Another good recipe for summertime when you really do not want a hot side dish for a picnic. This salad packs well once chilled, does not go flat, and is filling. Multi-colored pasta has a different nutritional value than plain macaroni because the green is usually made from spinach, and the orange is made from carrot flour. It is also prettier. The only heat produced from this dish is from cooking the pasta. This keeps your kitchen cooler, which could save money for budget-conscious working moms.

Ingredients:
1 lb spiral macaroni or bow tie pasta, multicolored
1 lb fresh broccoli, chopped
6 green salad onions, chopped
1 tsp garlic salt (mixed into the salad)
1 large tomato, diced
1 jar pickled artichoke hearts
1 green pepper, diced
1 cup fresh basil, chopped
1 can black olives, drained
½ cup virgin olive oil
1 [6 oz] package sliced pepperoni or salami

Directions: Fill a 4-quart kettle with water, cooking on high heat until the water is at a rolling boil. Add macaroni and turn water on low heat. Cook the multicolored macaroni pasta for 11 minutes. Drain and rinse with cold water. If you cook the pasta too long, it will become mushy and sticky. Cold water stops the cooking process. Drain the pickled artichoke hearts and black olives. Chop up artichoke hearts into smaller pieces and add to salad. Chop up the sliced salami or pepperoni into smaller squares and add to salad. Add all remaining ingredients, including olive oil, and mix well. Chill for one hour. This helps the salad gain more flavor from the spices. Garnish with fresh basil. Serves 6-8 people.

Japanese Cucumber Salad

This is a traditional salad that is served in Japanese restaurants around the country, and in sushi bars. It goes extremely well with fish and is supposed to clean your taste buds before a meal. It is tart, even with rice vinegar, which is sweeter than most vinegars. You can add a tablespoon of honey if you want it sweeter. I have known a lot of sushi chefs from California to Missouri. This is one of their favorites, served before the sushi or teriyaki.

Ingredients:
3 large cucumbers
1 cup non-roasted sesame seed
1 [12 oz] bottle rice vinegar

Directions: Peel and slice cucumbers into thin round slices. Put in large bowl and add vinegar and sesame seeds. Let chill for one hour. Serves 8 in small bowls.

Pico De Gallo

This is a traditional Mexican condiment that almost every North American restaurant uses for tortilla chips. If is much better than the pre-made version in a jar, which tends to lack flavor and fresh vegetable crunch. There are a couple different versions, depending if you are in Baja, Northern, or Southern Mexico. The Northern version uses cabbage and carrots, like a spicy coleslaw. This recipe is a Baja traditional version. It is not too spicy and not too hot and great with tortilla chips. Another good dip for football parties or sleepovers.

Ingredients:
2 large fresh tomatoes, diced
1 large white onion, diced
1 medium to small pickled jalapeno, diced in very small pieces
1 tsp garlic salt
1 bunch fresh or frozen cilantro, diced up for one cup

Directions: Mix all ingredients up in a medium-sized bowl, chill, and serve with homemade or store-bought tortilla chips for a healthy and refreshing snack.

Pickled Italian Pepperoncinis

The first thing you need are fresh pepperoncinis, which are small, green, slightly spicy sweet peppers. I grow mine in a window in the winter and replant them in the garden in the summer. If you do this, you will end up with a small pepper tree. You can pickle pepperoncini peppers to be either sweet or spicy pickles, depending on your taste. If you do not grow your own, you can find these at an Italian market.

Ingredients:
1 cup vinegar (or rice vinegar if you prefer sweet pickled peppers)
½ tsp garlic salt
1 cup fresh whole pepperoncini peppers (about 8 large ones or 12 small ones)
1 [8 oz] canning jar

Directions: Heat all ingredients in a 1-quart saucepan until it boils. Let boil for 5 minutes, until fresh peppers are blanched. You do not want to overcook them, or they get mushy. Put into sterile canning jar, and cover with the vinegar brine. (To sterilize jars, put the jar and not the lid in the microwave for one minute. This kills the yeast and bacteria.) Seal jar and let cool. Keep in the refrigerator.

Spinach Walnut Cranberry Salad with Raspberry Vinaigrette

Some people do not like walnuts, as they are sometimes dry and tart. In that case, you can replace the walnuts with unsalted almonds, which are naturally sweeter. If you want a whole meal, you can add grilled skinless chicken breast slices on top. It is still delicious. I have included the recipe for Raspberry Vinaigrette in this recipe, which you will also find in the Secret Sauces chapter of this book. My husband likes the walnuts, and I prefer the almonds for a slightly sweeter flavor.

Ingredients:
1 lb bag fresh spinach leaves, without the stems
1 lb walnut halves or 1 lb unsalted almonds
10 oz dried cranberries [2 cups]
2 cups frozen raspberries
1 cup apple vinegar
¼ tsp salt

Directions: Put two cups of frozen raspberries in a 1-quart pan and heat until boiling. Turn heat down and cook on medium heat for 15 minutes, then remove from heat. Put raspberries and apple vinegar in a blender with salt, and frappe. Put in a cruet or measuring cup in the refrigerator to cool. Combine washed spinach, dried cranberries, and unsalted almonds or walnut halves and mix together in a large salad bowl. Put raspberry vinaigrette on the side or pour on top for dressing. Serves 4-6.

Salmon Salad

I got tired of tuna salad and this was a nice change. Salmon fishing season is in July, and sometimes you can get a whole half of a fish that is not filleted yet for a reasonable price. When I make grilled or broiled salmon, this is how I turn the leftover salmon into something different. Using leftovers in another dish is better for the budget of working parents and more satisfying for the family.

Ingredients:
½-1 lb salmon, cooked and chopped
½ cup mayonnaise
½ cup diced dill pickles
1 tsp dill spice
½ tsp garlic salt
Pepper to flavor

Directions: Combine all of the above ingredients in a bowl, mix well, and use on crackers for hors d'oeuvres or on bread for a salmon sandwich. Serves 4 people.

Tzatziki – Greek Cucumber Yogurt

This is a Mediterranean recipe, which is made differently in Albania, Turkey, and through-out the islands. This is the traditional Greek version and is served with pita bread and lamb as a condiment. In Turkey, I had a cucumber chilled soup that was made of tzatziki with added cold water and garnished with mint. It was very good.

Ingredients:
1 large cucumber, peeled and diced
2 tbsp dried dill
1 tsp garlic salt
1 quart Greek non-flavored yogurt

Directions: Mix all ingredients in a bowl and chill in the refrigerator. The longer it sits, the better it tastes, as it absorbs the dill and garlic flavors. Keeps well covered in the refrigerator. Serves 6 people as a side salad or dip for kabob.

A Glossary of Cooking Terms and Tips

This is a guide for those who want to be a good cook with some helpful hints and terms that you might not be familiar with unless you went to a chef's school. I also included a part on how to smoke meats, which I learned in Texas while I was stationed in San Antonio. I used to drive for miles, smelling a smokehouse and following the scent. The chefs were always helpful and pleased to tell me how they made their brisket or meats. It helps to ask questions while you are young and cute.

Terms	Definition
Alfredo	Italian term for a sauce made with Parmesan cheese.
Basil	The most common herb in Italian cooking, along with oregano.
Blintz	Similar to a crepe, usually filled with creme cheese or fruits and rolled around the filling.
Bloom	Used for yeast activation, "blooming" means a foamy mixture with bubbles.
Bouillabaisse	The beginnings of a sauce or flavor, usually a broth.
Broth	Water and flavoring, e.g., beef, chicken, pork.
Coriander	A spice used for sweetening Middle and Far East recipes. Also used to spice tea.
Corn starch	One of the best kept secrets in a kitchen for thickening a stew, soup, gravy, or sauce. Has to be added to cold water and dissolved first to thicken. It will lump if added to hot sauces or soups by itself.
Crepe	A thin French pancake made with more eggs than regular pancakes, crispy on the edges when done right.
Curry	A name for a group of spices used in the Caribbean, India,

and the Middle and Far East.
There are over 300 different
types of curry. Most common
ones are red curries and yellow.
The red curries can be super
hot and spicy. If unsure, best to
try it on the tip of your finger
before adding to any recipe.

Frappe — Blending or whipping up a
liquid or semi-liquid until it is
smooth and foamy.

Fennel or Fennel Seed — A very spicy seed from India
and used in Eastern foods.
Used in small amounts as a
substitute for black pepper in
Indian foods and spicy breads.
Hotter than black pepper.

Fillet — A thin slice of meat usually cut
from a fish or other meats with
a long thin fillet knife.

Fresh Herb Preservation — Most of the spices in America
are dried but do not taste half
as good as the fresh ones. If you
grow your own herbs, wash
them and put them in a freezer
bag in the freezer. The flavor is
better and when frozen, the
stems fall off when you crunch
them in your hands.

Lemon zest — Equivalent to grated lemon
peels.

Parfait	A fancy word for layered puddings, usually served in a tulip-type glass cup so the layers are visible.
Phalange	The action of using two fingers on one hand with the thumb on the opposing hand to create a rippled edge, used to seal pastry like pie shells.
Pre-freezing	This is a term used by prep chefs in large kitchens, where you dice the vegetables and freeze them beforehand. This works really well when you have too many green peppers or onions. They freeze well and if you dice them first, you can measure a cup or whatever you need for a recipe. Especially good for soups and sauces.
Roux	The base for a recipe, often made with oil, fat, and flour, with spices.
Rub	This is a seasoning made with spices and salt, used primarily for sealing in the flavor of meats when cooking. Kansas City style has more red cayenne and paprika. Monterey rub has garlic and salt with some black pepper. Cajun rub is red-hot-

spicy but goes well with a sweet barbecue sauce. Jalapeño rub has cilantro and garlic, best used with lime or lemon marinade.

Yeast   A fungus that makes bread rise. If you want sourdough, ale, beer, or cheese, it takes a different form of yeast, a different subspecies.

How to Smoke Meats

This is one of the best kept secrets of a "humadora," the Spanish word for a smoking chef. Many chefs will not tell you how to smoke your chicken or pork. I learned this in Texas when I was very young. If your meat is tough, like a brisket, you might want to cook it on low heat in the oven first for about 6 hours, or until you can cut it with a fork. (See No Work Brisket recipe.) Chicken, fish, and pork, if tender, do not need to be pre-cooked. If ribs are tough, I still put them in the oven first, so they fall off the bone when they are smoked. This is called a double-cooked recipe. Smoking is easier if you have a temperature-controlled grill. However, I do this on a little grill, and it works fine as long as you have a grill cover. I use hickory wood chips because I like the flavor, but you can use applewood or mesquite wood chips if you prefer. They are a little milder. After I smoke the meat, I then add a layer of barbecue sauce and let them heat up again. This makes the third cooking stage.

Ingredients:
2 tbsp your favorite meat rub
3-4 lbs your favorite raw meat (if using ribs, use two racks)
2 cups wood chips
4 cups water
5 cups charcoal

Directions: Meat rub is used to hold the flavors and juices in the meat. Spread the rub over the surface of the meat until it is well covered. Usually meat rub has the spices including salt that add flavor, so it is also a seasoning. Get your coals started and leave until medium hot, usually a half hour. While the coals are heating, put the wood chips in the water and let them soak. I usually let the wood chips sit in the morning until I need them. The wetter the wood chips, the slower they will burn.

You can smoke meats on a low flame or a medium flame if you are cooking the meat. High flames will burn the wood and the meat. Once the coals are ready, lay your rubbed meat on the top of a large cookie sheet or foil. I have a cookie sheet that I use for smoking meats only. It has developed a brown patina which can't be scrubbed off. I put the foil or cookie sheet separately on the grill, and not directly on the flame over the charcoal. This prevents having a messy grill to clean up later. Add soaked wood chips directly on top of the coals and put your foil and meat away from the center of the flame on the grill. Cover grill and let air in by the vents so your fire does not go out. Let smoke until the meat is done and is turning slightly pink from the smoke. This takes at least 30 minutes on each side. Then, turn the meat over to smoke the other side. If your hickory burns up, add another cup of wet woodchips to the hot coals.

When the meat is cooked, add your favorite barbecue sauce and cover top of the meat. I use Granny's Barbecue Sauce, found in the Secret Sauces chapter of this book. It will not drip or run off of the meat like the store-bought brands. Turn the meat over in 30 minutes and coat the other side of the meat with barbecue sauce. You will never buy another jar of runny, watered-down barbecue sauce again. Serves 6 people unless they really like smoked ribs. I have a couple of friends who can eat a whole rack by themselves, so I double the recipe. This is what your meats should look like after being smoked and sauced. See photo below.

How to Cook Venison so it is Tender and Tasty

While stationed in Texas, I ate some venison which I think was sold by Uniroyal tire company. It was the toughest meat I have ever eaten. I learned how to cook venison in Wisconsin on a farm. I went home that Christmas to inquire about how to cook this delicious low-fat, low-cholesterol dish. My Uncle Bruce taught me a few secrets after hunting season. First, it does matter how you prepare the meat. Using a very sharp fillet knife, cut off all the fascia, the thin lining of muscle and tendon that covers the meat. It will shrink with heat and make it tougher. If your meat is too "wild tasting," add a shot or two of whiskey. The alcohol will cook out and it kills the wild taste. Cook on low heat in the oven for 3-4 hours at 180 degrees Fahrenheit, using a coating of meat rub, and cover with barbecue sauce. I prefer my granny's barbecue sauce. Your children will never know they are eating "Bambi," and it will not be tough and chewy.

About Atmosphere Press

Atmosphere Press is an independent, full-service publisher for excellent books in all genres and for all audiences. Learn more about what we do at atmospherepress.com.

We encourage you to check out some of Atmosphere's latest releases, which are available at Amazon.com and via order from your local bookstore:

Carlito the Bat Learns to Trick-or-Treat, a picture book by Michele Lizet Flores

Waking Up Marriage: Finding Truth In Your Partnership, nonfiction by Bill O'Herron

Eat to Lead, nonfiction by Luci Gabel

An Ambiguous Grief, a memoir by Dominique Hunter

For a Better Life, a novel by Julia Reid Galosy

GROW: A Jack and Lake Creek Book, a novel by Chris S McGee

Whose Mary Kate, a novel by Jane Leclere Doyle

You are the Moon, a picture book by Shana Rachel Diot

In the Cloakroom of Proper Musings, a lyric narrative by Kristina Moriconi

The Glorious Between, a novel by Doug Reid

Skinny Vanilla Crisis, a novel by Colleen Alles

The Mommy Clique, a novel by Barbara Altamirano

Olive, a novel by Barbara Braendlein

Eyeless Mind, nonfiction by Stephanie Duesing

White Snake Diary, nonfiction by Jane P. Perry

About the Author

Rebecca Cailor is a retired nurse practitioner with 35 years of nursing experience and 42 years of cooking experience.

She was a single mother for 10 years. She worked in remote areas around the United States and collected various recipes while working in these areas and while traveling to other countries. Instead of bringing back souvenirs, she brought back recipes and local spices from her travels to enchant her sons with new flavors and nutritious meals.

Raising two boys through nursing school and while working two jobs is a challenge for anybody. She created these recipes for the most finicky eaters and is very aware of the challenges for raising a family while working. She is now retired in Panama, Central America and enjoys cooking meals for her friends and creating new flavors.

CPSIA information can be obtained
at www.ICGtesting.com
Printed in the USA
LVHW072014050221
678489LV00016B/1646

9 781636 495606